HTML, XHTML & CSS FOR DUMMIES

KU-623-363

6th Edition

Named Colors and Hex Values

Name	Hexcode		Name	Hexcode	
aqua	#00FFFF		navy	#000080	
black	#000000		olive	#808000	
blue	#0000FF		purple	#800080	
fuchsia	#FF00FF		red	#FF0000	
gray	#808080		silver	#C0C0C0	
green	#008000		teal	#008080	
lime	#00FF00		white	#FFFFFF	
maroon	#800000		yellow	#FFFF00	

Web Safe Colors

#000000	#0000FF	#0033CC	#0066CC	#009999
#0099FF	#00CCCC	#00FFFF	#330000	#3300FF
#333300	#336600	#3366FF	#3399FF	#33CCFF
#33FFFF	#660000	#663300	#6633FF	#666600
#666666	#669900	#669966	#66CCCC	#66FFFF
#990000	#993300	#993333	#996600	#9966FF
#999900	#99CC00	#99FF66	#99FFCC	#CC0000
#CC00FF	#CC3300	#CC33FF	#CC66CC	#CC9999
#CCCCCC	#CCCCFF	#CCFFCC	#FF00CC	#FF33CC
#FF33FF	#FF66CC	#FF9999	#FFCCCC	#FFCCFF
#FFFFCC	#FFFFFF			

HTML Elements

Element	Common Name	Empty	Deprecated	Category	Description
`<!-- ... -->`	Comment	Neither	No	Doc structure	Instructs HTML parser to ignore text comments in document
`<!doctype>`	Document type	Neither	No	Doc structure	(X)HTML document type definition; first element in all such docs
`abbr`	Abbreviation	No	No	Text element	Flags abbreviated text
`acronym`	Acronym	No	No	Text element	Flags acronyms
`address`	Address	No	No	Doc structure	Identify document author, contact information
`blockquote`	Blockquote	No	No	Text element	Sets off long quotations from body text

For Dummies: Bestselling Book Series for Beginners

HTML, XHTML & CSS
FOR DUMMIES
6th Edition

Cheat Sheet

HTML Elements *(continued)*

Element	Common Name	Empty	Deprecated	Category	Description
body	Document body	No	No	Doc structure	Identifies (X)HTML document body
br	Line break	Yes	No	Text element	Forces line break in document text
cite	Citation	No	No	Text element	Identifies information source or reference
code	Code	No	No	Text element	Identifies computer code/script fragment
dd	Definition description	No	No	List element	Identifies definition text in list of definitions or glossary
del	Deleted text	No	No	Text element	Marks enclosed text as deleted from current document version
dfn	Term definition	No	No	Text element	Marks terms the first time they appear in a document with a definition
div	Document division	No	No	Doc structure	Marks logical divisions in a document, groups block level elements
dl	Definition list	No	No	List element	Encloses definition elements (dt and dd) in a definition list
dt	Definition term	No	No	List element	Identifies term being defined in a definition list
em	Emphasis	No	No	Text element	Provides typographic emphasis, usually rendered in italics
h1, h2, ..., h6	Header levels 1 thru 6	No	No	Doc structure	Identifies heading level hierarchy six levels deep
head	Document head	No	No	Doc structure	Contains markup for (X)HTML document head
html	HTML document	No	No	Doc structure	Encloses (X)HTML document head and body elements
ins	Inserted text	No	No	Text element	Marks enclosed text as inserted into current document version
li	List item	No	No	List element	Identifies item inside an (X)HTML list type: dir, menu, ol, ul
meta	Meta information	Yes	No	Doc structure	Use inside head to describe document contents, markup, etc.
ol	Ordered list	No	No	List element	List style that numbers included elements in order of appearance
p	Paragraph	No	No	Text element	Forms enclosed text into individual paragraphs
pre	Preformatted text	No	No	Text element	Preserves original formatting, indentation and white space of text
q	Quotation	No	No	Text element	Used to highlight short quotations from other sources
span	Localizes style/format	No	No	Doc structure	Applies style information to text within a document
strong	Strong emphasis	No	No	Text element	Strong visual emphasis for key words/phrases within normal doc text
sub	Subscript	No	No	Text element	Render enclosed text as a subscript, lower than surrounding text
sup	Superscript	No	No	Text element	Render enclosed text as a superscript, higher than surrounding text
title	Document title	No	No	Doc structure	head element that titles a document (shows in browser title bar)
ul	Unordered list	No	No	List element	List items enclosed show up in a bulleted list in order of appearance

For Dummies: Bestselling Book Series for Beginners

HTML, XHTML & CSS

FOR

DUMMIES®

6th Edition

by Ed Tittel and Jeff Noble

WILEY

Wiley Publishing, Inc.

HTML, XHTML & CSS For Dummies®, 6th Edition

Published by
Wiley Publishing, Inc.
111 River Street
Hoboken, NJ 07030-5774

www.wiley.com

For general information on our other products and services, please contact our Customer Care Department within the U.S. at 800-762-2974, outside the U.S. at 317-572-3993, or fax 317-572-4002.

For technical support, please visit www.wiley.com/techsupport.

Wiley also publishes its books in a variety of electronic formats. Some content that appears in print may not be available in electronic books.

Library of Congress Control Number: 2008924086

ISBN: 978-0-470-23847-9

Manufactured in the United States of America

10 9 8 7 6 5 4 3 2 1

WILEY

About the Authors

Ed Tittel is a full-time independent writer, trainer, and consultant who works out of his home near beautiful Austin, Texas. Ed has been writing for the trade press since 1986 and has worked on more than 140 books. In addition to this title, Ed has worked on more than 35 books for Wiley, including *Windows Server 2008 For Dummies, XML For Dummies,* and *Networking with NetWare For Dummies.*

Ed is a Contributing Editor at Tomshardware.com, writes for half-a-dozen different TechTarget.com Web sites, including WhatIs.com, SearchNetworking.com, and SearchWindows.com, and also writes occasionally for other Web sites and magazines. When he's not busy doing all that work stuff, Ed likes to travel, shoot pool, spend time with his family (especially taking walks with young Gregory), and turn the tables on his Mom, who now makes her home with the rest of the Texas Tittels.

You can contact Ed Tittel by e-mail at `etittel@yahoo.com`.

Jeff Noble runs a small Web design and multimedia company called Conquest Media (`www.conquestmedia.com`) in Austin, Texas. Jeff has been working on, in, and around the Web for nearly 10 years, and he specializes in designing and creating unique, easy to use, functional Web sites. When he's away from his computer, Jeff is often far from the madding crowd, choosing instead to hike and camp in wild places as far away from a wall socket as he can get.

Jeff is available for Web site design, implementation, and consulting work. You can contact him by e-mail at `jeff@conquestmedia.com`.

Authors' Acknowledgments

Now that we've made it into the twelfth go-round for *HTML For Dummies,* we must once again thank our many readers for keeping this book alive. We'd also like to thank them and the Wiley editors for providing the feedback that drives the continuing improvement of this book. Please don't stop now — tell us what you want to do, and what you like and don't like about this book. Especially, please tell us what you liked and didn't like about this, our first full-color edition of our book.

Let me also thank the many people who've also worked on this book over the years, including James Michael Stewart, Natanya Anderson, Dori Smith, Tom Negrino, Mary Burmeister, Rich Wagner, Brock Kyle, Chelsea Valentine, and Kim Lindros. Of course, for this edition, I'm especially indebted to my co-author and friend, Jeff Noble, for infusing insight and enthusiasm into this book. I am eternally grateful to you for your ideas, your hard work, and your experience in reaching an audience of budding Web experts.

Next, I'd like to thank the Wiley team for their efforts on this title. At Wiley, I must thank Bob Woerner and Paul Levesque for their outstanding efforts, and Barry Childs-Helton and Sue Jenkins for their editorial efforts in design, layout, contents, and coverage. A special shout out should go to the friendly folks in Composition Services for their artful page layouts, especially when it came to keeping all the color-coded code straight.

I'd like to thank my lovely wife, Dina Kutueva-Tittel, and periodically pugnacious 4-year-old son, Gregory, for putting up with the usual rhythm of making books happen. I know I'm not always as easy to live with as I should be, but hopefully, I'll get to keep working on that. Also, I'd like to thank my parents, Al and Ceil, for all the great things they did for me, and for hanging in there well into their ninth decades on this planet. I hope you're both still around to see the thirteenth edition come to print as well! Finally, profound thanks to you again, Mom, for cultivating and encouraging my love of words, writing, and banter.

Ed Tittel

First and foremost, I'd like to thank my mom, Sheryl, for always believing in me. I'd like to thank my older brother Chris, even though he once shot me with his BB gun when we were kids. (I'd also like to mention that one year for Christmas he gave me a used Skid Row tape made to look semi-new covered with Saran Wrap. But I've moved past that.) Thanks again, bro. To my "adopted" family, The Elizondos, I appreciate everything you have done for me over the years and I promise to never sing Christmas carols in the house. *"Shut up Jeff!"*

I'd certainly like to thank Ed Tittel for giving a semi-literate guy such as myself this opportunity: you're a good friend, a great writer, and definitely know a thing or two about local Austin eateries.

I want to give special thanks to the following friends and colleagues: Slade Deliberto for teaching me how to design Web sites, Matt "Softball" Douglass for convincing me CSS is a lot better than old school HTML tags, Justin Haworth for bailing me out of many confusing Flash scripting problems, Peter "3D Pete" Vogel for his mentoring and assistance creating the Conquest Media logo, Jason "GodLikeMouse" Graves for teaching me almost everything I know about JavaScript, XML and CSS layout, and Russell Wilson for his usability lessons and expert advice. Thanks to the whole gang at Conquest Media, too!

Jeff Noble

Publisher's Acknowledgments

We're proud of this book; please send us your comments through our Dummies Online Registration Form located at www.dummies.com.

Some of the people who helped bring this book to market include the following:

Acquisitions, Editorial, and Media Development

Project Editor: Paul Levesque

Acquisitions Editor: Bob Woerner

Copy Editor: Barry Childs-Helton

Technical Editor: Sue Jenkins

Editorial Manager: Leah Cameron

Media Development Supervisor: Richard Graves

Editorial Assistant: Amanda Foxworth

Cartoons: Rich Tennant, www.the5thwave.com

Production

Project Coordinator: Katie Key

Layout and Graphics: Kathie Rickard, Erin Zeltner

Proofreaders: Betty Kish, Dwight Ramsey, Toni Settle

Indexer: Ty Koontz

Publishing and Editorial for Technology Dummies

Richard Swadley, Vice President and Executive Group Publisher

Andy Cummings, Vice President and Publisher

Mary Bednarek, Executive Acquisitions Director

Mary C. Corder, Editorial Director

Publishing for Consumer Dummies

Diane Graves Steele, Vice President and Publisher

Joyce Pepple, Acquisitions Director

Composition Services

Gerry Fahey, Vice President of Production Services

Debbie Stailey, Director of Composition Services

Contents at a Glance

Table of Contents

Introduction

*W*elcome to the wild, wacky, and wonderful possibilities of the World Wide Web, more simply called *the Web*. In this book, we reveal the mysteries of the markup languages that are the lifeblood of the Web — the Hypertext Markup Language (HTML) and its successor, XHTML, along with the Cascading Style Sheet (CSS) language widely used to make the other stuff look good. Because HTML and XHTML (we use *(X)HTML* in this book to refer to both versions at once) and CSS may be used to build Web pages, learning how to use them brings you into the fold of Web authors and content developers.

If you've tried to build your own Web pages but found it too forbidding, now you can relax. If you can dial a telephone or find your keys in the morning, you too can become an (X)HTML author. No kidding!

This book keeps the technobabble to a minimum and sticks with plain English whenever possible. Besides plain talk about hypertext, (X)HTML, and the Web, we include lots of examples, plus tag-by-tag instructions to help you build your very own Web pages with minimum muss and fuss. We also provide more examples about what to do with your Web pages after they're created so you can share them with the world. We also explain the differences between HTML 4 and XHTML, so you can decide whether you want to stick with the best-known and longest-lived Web markup language (HTML) or its later and greater successor (XHTML).

We also have a companion Web site for this book that contains (X)HTML and CSS examples from the chapters in usable form — plus pointers to interesting widgets that you can use to embellish your own documents and astound your friends. Visit `www.edtittel.com/html4d6e` and start browsing from there.

About This Book

Think of this book as a friendly, approachable guide to taking up the tools of (X)HTML and CSS, and building readable, attractive pages for the Web. These things aren't hard to learn, but they pack a lot of details. You must handle at least some of these details as you build your own Web pages. Topics you find in this book include

✔ Designing and building Web pages

✔ Uploading and publishing Web pages for the world to see

✔ Testing and debugging your Web pages

You can build Web pages without years of arduous training, advanced aesthetic capabilities, or ritual ablutions in ice-cold streams. If you can tell somebody how to drive across town to your house, you can build a useful Web document. The purpose of this book isn't to turn you into a rocket scientist (or, for that matter, a rocket scientist into a Web site). The purpose is to show you the design and technical elements you need for a good-looking, readable Web page and to give you the confidence to do it!

How to Use This Book

This book tells you how to use (X)HTML and CSS to get your Web pages up and running on the World Wide Web. We tell you what's involved in designing and building effective Web documents that can bring your ideas and information to the whole online world — if that's what you want to do — and maybe have some high-tech fun communicating them.

All (X)HTML and CSS code appears in monospaced type like this:

```
<head><title>What's in a Title?</title></head>...
```

When you type (X)HTML tags, CSS, or other related information, be sure to copy the information exactly as you see it between the angle brackets (< and >), including the angle brackets themselves, because that's part of the magic that makes (X)HTML and CSS work. Other than that, you find out how to marshal and manage the content that makes your pages special, and we tell you exactly what you need to do to mix the elements of (X)HTML and CSS with your own work.

The margins of a book don't give us the same room as the vast reaches of cyberspace. Therefore, some long lines of (X)HTML and CSS markup, or designations for Web sites (called *URLs,* for *Uniform Resource Locators*), may wrap to the next line. Remember that your computer shows such wrapped lines as a *single line of (X)HTML or CSS,* or as a single URL — so if you type that hunk of code, keep it as one line. Don't insert a hard return if you see one of these wrapped lines. We clue you in that the (X)HTML or CSS markup is supposed to be *all one line* by breaking the line at a slash or other appropriate character (to imply "but wait, there's more!") and by slightly indenting the overage, as in the following silly example:

```
http://www.infocadabra.transylvania.com/nexus/plexus/lexus/
      praxis/okay/this/is/a/make-believe/URL/but/some/real/
      ones/are/SERIOUSLY/long.html
```

HTML doesn't care whether you type tag text in uppercase, lowercase, or both (except for character entities, also known as character codes). XHTML and CSS, however, want tag text only in lowercase to be perfectly correct. Thus, to make your own work look like ours as much as possible, enter all (X) HTML and CSS tag text, and all other code, *in lowercase only*. (If you have a prior edition of the book, this reverses our earlier instructions. The keepers of the eternal and ever-magnanimous standard of HTML, the World Wide Web Consortium (W3C), have restated the rules, so we follow their lead. We don't make the rules, but we *do* know how to play the game!)

You'll also find that our code listings are color coded, where we assign specific colors to various types of markup. This is explained in Chapter 1 in a sidebar titled "Markup Color Coding." (You might notice that all the illustrations have nice, pretty colors, too!)

Three Presumptuous Assumptions

They say that making assumptions makes a fool out of the person who makes them and the person who is subject to those assumptions (and just who are *they,* anyway? We *assume* we know, but . . . never mind).

You don't need to be a master logician or a wizard in the arcane arts of programming, nor do you need a Ph.D. in computer science. You don't even need a detailed sense of what's going on in the innards of your computer to deal with the material in this book.

Even so, practicality demands that we make a few assumptions about you, gentle reader: You can turn your computer on and off; you know how to use a mouse and a keyboard; and you want to build your own Web pages for fun, profit, or your job. We also assume that you already have a working connection to the Internet and a Web browser.

If you can write a sentence and know the difference between a heading and a paragraph, you can build and publish your own documents on the Web. The rest consists of details — and we help you with those!

How This Book Is Organized

This book contains six major parts, arranged like Russian *Matrioshka* (nesting dolls). Parts contain at least three chapters, and each chapter contains several modular sections. That way you can use this book to

✔ Jump around.

✔ Find topics or keywords in the Index or in the Table of Contents.

✔ Read the whole book from cover to cover.

Part 1: Getting to Know (X)HTML and CSS

This part sets the stage and includes an overview of and introduction to the Web and the software that people use to mine its treasures. This section also explains how the Web works, including the (X)HTML and CSS that this book covers, and the server-side software and services that deliver the goods to end users (when we aren't preoccupied with the innards of our systems).

(X)HTML documents, also called *Web pages,* are the fundamental units of information organization and delivery on the Web. Here you also discover what HTML is about, how hypertext can enrich ordinary text, and what CSS does to modify and manage how that text looks on display. Next you take a walk on the Web side and build your very first (X)HTML document.

Part 11: Formatting Web Pages with (X)HTML

HTML mixes ordinary text with special strings of characters called *markup,* used to instruct browsers how to display (X)HTML documents. In this part of the book, you find out about markup in general and (X)HTML in particular. We start with a fascinating discussion of (X)HTML document organization and structure. (Well . . . *we* think it's fascinating, and hope you do, too.) Next we explain how text can be organized into blocks and lists. Then we tackle how the hyperlinks that put the *H* into (X)HTML work. After that, we discuss how you can find and use graphical images in your Web pages and make some fancy formatting maneuvers to spruce up those pages.

Throughout this part of the book, we include discussion of (X)HTML markup elements *(tags)* and how they work. By the time you finish Part II, expect to have a good overall idea of what HTML is and how you can use it.

Part 111: Taking Precise Control Over Web Pages and Styles

Part III starts with a discussion of Cascading Style Sheets (CSS) — another form of markup language that lets (X)HTML deal purely with content while it deals with how Web pages look when they're displayed in a Web browser or as rendered on other devices (PDAs, mobile phones, and special so-called assistive devices for print-handicapped users). After exploring CSS syntax and structures and discovering how to use them, you find out how to manipulate the color and typefaces of text, backgrounds, and more on your Web pages. You also learn about more complex collections of markup — specifically tables — as you explore and observe their capabilities in detail. We give you lots of examples to help you design and build commercial-grade (X)HTML documents. You can get started working with related (X)HTML tag syntax and structures that you need to know so you can build complex Web pages.

Part IV: Integrating Scripts with (X)HTML

(X)HTML isn't good at snazzing up text and graphics when they're on display (that's where CSS excels). And (X)HTML really can't *do* much by itself. Web designers often build interactive, dynamic Web pages by using scripting tools to add interactivity to an (X)HTML framework.

In this part of the book, you find out about scripting languages that enable Web pages to interact with users and that also provide ways to respond to user input or actions and to grab and massage data along the way. You get introduced to general scripting languages, and we jump directly into the most popular of such languages — JavaScript. You can discover the basic elements of this scripting language and how to add interactivity to Web pages. You can also explore typical uses for scripting that you can extend and add to your own Web site. We go on to explore how to create and extract data from Web-based data input forms and how to create and use scripts that react to a user's actions while she visits your Web pages.

Throughout this part of the book, examples, advice, and details show you how these scripting components can enhance and improve your Web site's capabilities — and your users' experiences when visiting your pages.

Part V: (X)HTML Projects

This part tackles typical complex Web pages. You can use these as models for similar capabilities in your own Web pages. These projects include personal and company pages, an eBay auction page, and even a product catalog page with its own shopping cart!

Part VI: The Part of Tens

We sum up and distill the very essence of the mystic secrets of (X)HTML. Here you can read further about cool Web tools, get a second chance to review top dos and don'ts for HTML markup, and review how to catch and kill potential bugs and errors in your pages before anybody else sees them. You also get a collection of killer online resources you can use to further your own ongoing education in HTML, XHTML, and CSS over time.

Icons Used in This Book

 This icon signals technical details that are informative and interesting but aren't absolutely critical to writing HTML.

 This icon flags useful information that makes HTML markup or other important stuff even less complicated than you feared it might be.

 This icon points out information you shouldn't pass by — don't overlook these gentle reminders (the life, sanity, or page you save could be your own).

 Be cautious when you see this icon. It warns you of things you shouldn't do; consequences can be severe if you ignore the accompanying bit of wisdom.

 Text marked with this icon contains information about something that can be found on this book's companion Web site. You can find all the code examples in this book, for starters. Simply visit our Web site for this book at `www.edtittel.com/html4d6e`, and look for pointers to examples, templates, and more. We also use this icon to point out some great and useful Web resources.

 The information highlighted with this icon gives best practices — advice that we wish we'd had when we first started out! These techniques can save you time and money on migraine medication.

Where to Go from Here

This is where you pick a direction and hit the road! Where you start out doesn't matter. Don't worry. You can handle it. Who cares whether anybody else thinks you're just goofing around? We know you're getting ready to have the time of your life. Enjoy!

Part I

Getting to Know (X)HTML and CSS

The 5th Wave   By Rich Tennant

"You know, I've asked you a dozen times NOT to animate the torches on our Web site."

In this part . . .

In this part of the book, we explore and explain basic HTML document links and structures. We also explain the key role that Web browsers play in delivering all this stuff to people's desktops. We even explain where the *(X)* comes from — namely, a reworking of the original description of HTML markup using XML syntax to create XHTML — and go on to help you understand what makes XHTML different (and possibly better, according to some) than plain old HTML. We also take a look at general Web-page anatomy, at the various pieces and parts that make up a Web page, and at how CSS helps to manage their presentation, placement, and even color when they appear on somebody's display.

Next, we take you through the exercise of creating and viewing a simple Web page so you can understand what's involved in doing this for yourself. We also explain what's involved in making changes to an existing Web page and how to post your changes (or a new page) online.

This part concludes with a rousing exhortation to figure out what you're doing before making too much markup happen. Just as a well-built house starts with a set of blueprints and architectural drawings, so should a Web page (and site) start with a plan or a map, with some idea of where your pages will reside in cyberspace and how hordes of users can find their way to them.

Chapter 1

The Least You Need to Know about HTML, CSS, and the Web

*W*elcome to the wonderful world of the Web, (X)HTML, and CSS. With just a little knowledge, some practice, and something to say, you can either build your own little piece of cyberspace or expand on work you've already done.

This book is your down-and-dirty guide to putting together your first Web page, sprucing up an existing Web page, or creating complex and exciting pages that integrate intricate designs, multimedia, and scripting.

The best way to start working with HTML is to jump right in, so that's what this chapter does: It brings you up to speed on the basics of how (X)HTML and CSS work behind the scenes of Web pages, introducing you to their underlying building blocks. When you're done with this chapter, you'll know how (X)HTML and CSS work so you can start creating Web pages right now.

Web Pages in Their Natural Habitat

Web pages can accommodate many kinds of content, such as *text, graphics, forms, audio and video files,* and *interactive games.*

Browse the Web for just a little while and you see a buffet of information and content displayed in many ways. Every Web site is different, but most have one thing in common: Hypertext Markup Language (HTML). You'll also run into XHTML and Cascading Style Sheets (CSS) pretty regularly too.

Whatever information a Web page contains, every Web page is created in HTML (or some reasonable facsimile). HTML is the mortar that holds a Web page together; the graphics, content, and other information are the bricks; CSS tells Web pages how they should look when on display.

HTML files that produce Web pages are just text documents, as are XHTML and CSS files. That's why the Web works as well as it does. Text is a universal language for computers. Any text file you create on a Windows computer — including any HTML, XHTML, or CSS file — works equally well on a Mac or any other operating system.

But Web pages aren't *merely* text documents. They're made with special, attention-deprived, sugar-loaded text called *HTML, XHTML,* or *CSS.* Each uses its own specific set of instructions that you include (along with your content) inside text files that specify how a page should look and behave.

Stick with us to discover all the details you need to know about (X)HTML and CSS!

When we say (X)HTML, we're really talking about HTML and XHTML together. Although they're not identical, they're enough like each other for this kind of reference to make sense.

Hypertext

Special instructions in HTML permit lines of text to point (that is, *link*) to something else in cyberspace. Such pointers are called *hyperlinks.* Hyperlinks are the glue that holds the World Wide Web together. In your Web browser, hyperlinks usually appear in blue and are underlined. When you click one, it takes you somewhere else.

Hypertext or not, a Web page is a text file, which means you can create and edit a Web page in any application that creates plain text (such as Notepad or TextEdit). Some software tools offer fancy options and applications (covered in Chapter 22) to help you create Web pages, but they generate the same text files that you create with plain-text editors. We're of the opinion, though, that those just getting started with HTML are best served by a simple text editor. Just break out Notepad on the PC (or TextEdit on the Mac) and you're ready to go.

Steer clear of word processors like WordPad or MS Word for creating HTML because they introduce all kinds of extra code on Web pages that you may neither want nor need.

Figure 1-3:
The com-
ponents of
a URL help
it define the
exact loca-
tion of a file
on the Web.

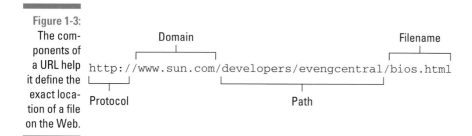

Figure 1-3:
The components of a URL help it define the exact location of a file on the Web.

Domain

Filename

`http://www.sun.com/developers/evengcentral/bios.html`

Protocol

Path

Each URL component helps define the location of a Web page or resource:

- **Protocol:** Specifies the protocol the browser follows to request the file.

  The Web page protocol is `http://` (the usual start to most URLs).

- **Domain:** Points to the general Web site (such as `www.sun.com`) where the file resides. A domain may host a few files (like a personal Web site) or millions of files (like a corporate site, such as `www.sun.com`).

- **Path:** Names the sequence of folders through which you must navigate to get to a specific file.

  For example, to get to a file in the `evangcentral` folder that resides in the `developers` folder, you use the `/developers/evangcentral/` path.

- **Filename:** Specifies which file in a directory path the browser accesses.

Although the URL shown in Figure 1-3 is no longer publicly accessible, it points to the Sun domain and offers a path that leads to a specific file named `bios.html`:

    http://www.sun.com/developers/evangcentral/bios.html

Chapter 6 provides the complete details on how you use HTML and URLs to add hyperlinks to your Web pages, and Chapter 3 shows how to obtain a URL for your own Web site after you're ready move it to a Web server.

(X)HTML's Component Parts

The following section removes the mystery from the *X*. This section shows

- The differences between HTML and XHTML
- How HTML is written (its *syntax*)
- Rules that govern its use

    ✔ Names for important pieces and parts of HTML (and XHTML) markup

    ✔ How to make the best, most correct use of (X)HTML capabilities

HTML and XHTML: What's the difference?

HTML is *Hypertext Markup Language,* a notation developed in the late 1980s and early 1990s for describing Web pages. HTML is now enshrined in numerous standard descriptions (*specifications*) from the World Wide Web Consortium (W3C). The last HTML specification was finalized in 1999.

When you put an *X* in front of *HTML* to get *XHTML,* you get a new, improved version of HTML based on the *eXtensible Markup Language (XML).* XML is designed to work and behave well with computers, software, and the Internet.

The original formulation of HTML has some irregularities that can cause heartburn for software that reads HTML documents. XHTML, on the other hand, uses an extremely regular and predictable syntax that's easier for software to handle. XHTML will replace HTML someday, but HTML keeps on ticking. This book covers both varieties and shows you the steps to put the X in front of your own HTML documents and turn them into XHTML.

Introducing Internet protocols

Interactions between browsers and servers are made possible by a set of computer-communication instructions: Hypertext Transfer Protocol (HTTP). This protocol defines how browsers should request Web pages and how Web servers should respond to those requests.

HTTP isn't the only protocol at work on the Internet. The Simple Mail Transfer Protocol (SMTP) and Post Office Protocol (POP) make e-mail exchange possible, and the File Transfer Protocol (FTP) allows you to upload, download, move, copy, and delete files and folders across the Internet. The good news is that Web browsers and servers do all the HTTP work for you, so you only have to put your pages on a server or type a Web address into a browser.

To see how HTTP works, check out David Gourley and Brian Totty's chapter on HTTP messages, available through Google book search with "understanding http transactions" as the search string. Start your search at `http://google.books.com`, then scroll down until you see the link to "HTTP: The Definitive Guide – Page 80."

✔ Most HTML and XHTML markup are identical.

✔ In a few cases, HTML and XHTML markup look a little different.

✔ In a few cases, HTML and XHTML markup must be used differently.

This book shows how to create code that works in both HTML and XHTML.

Syntax and rules

HTML is a straightforward language for describing Web page contents. XHTML is even less demanding. Their components are easy to use — when you know how to use a little bit of (X)HTML. Both HTML and XHTML markup have three types of components:

✔ **Elements:** Identify different parts of an HTML page by using tags

✔ **Attributes:** Information about an instance of an element

✔ **Entities:** Non-ASCII text characters, such as copyright symbols (©) and accented letters (É). Entities originate from the Standard Generic Markup Language, or SGML.

Every bit of HTML and/or XHTML markup that describes a Web page's content includes some combination of elements, attributes, and entities.

Markup color coding

As we present HTML, XHTML, and CSS information in our code samples, we use color coding to help you distinguish what's what by way of markup. Here is a color key that you should keep in mind as you read all of our code listings.

Purple: indicates the DOCTYPE declaration used in (X)HTML documents. This is actually a totally different markup language known as the Standard Generalized Markup Language, or SGML. It is used to identify what specific set of rules that (X)HTML documents follow in their construction and content. It also applies to codes for character entities, which take the form &pos; or &123;.

Light Green: indicates ordinary garden variety XHTML and HTML markup

Dark Green: indicates XML markup

Orange: indicates Cascading Style Sheet, or CSS, markup

Blue: indicates JavaScript

We only colorize markup in code listings, because it affects readability too much when code appears in body copy. In that case, we simply use a different, monospaced font — as you'll see in the discussions of the `<html>`, `<head>`, and `<title>` elements in our first paragraph that discusses HTML markup here.

This chapter covers the basic form and syntax for elements, attributes, and entities. Parts II and III of the book detail how elements and attributes:

- Describe kinds of text (such as paragraphs or tables)
- Create an effect on the page (such as changing a font style)
- Add images and links to a page

Elements

Elements are the building blocks of (X)HTML. You use them to describe every piece of text on your page. Elements are made up of tags and the content within those tags. There are two main types of elements:

- Elements with content made up of a tag pair and whatever content sits between the opening and closing tag in the pair
- Elements that insert something into the page, using a single tag

Tag pairs

Elements that describe content use a *tag pair* to mark the beginning and the end of the element. Start and end tag pairs look like this:

```
<tag>...</tag>
```

Content — such as paragraphs, headings, tables, and lists — always uses a tag pair:

- The start tag (`<tag>`) tells the browser, "The element begins here."
- The end tag (`</tag>`) tells the browser, "The element ends here."

The actual content is what occurs between the start tag and end tag. For example, the Ed Tittel page in Listing 1-1 uses the paragraph element (`<p>`) to surround the text of a paragraph (we omit CSS inline markup for clarity):

```
<p>Ed started writing about computing subjects in 1986 for a
 Macintosh oriented monthly magazine. By 1989 he had contributed to such
publications as LAN Times, Network World, Mac World, and LAN Magazine. He worked
on his first book in 1991, and by 1994 had contributed to over a dozen different
titles.</p>
```

Single tags

Elements that insert something into the page are called *empty elements* (because they enclose no content) and use just a single tag, like this:

```
<tag />
```

Images and line breaks insert something into the HTML file, so they use one tag.

One key difference between XHTML and HTML is that, in XHTML, all empty elements must end with a slash before the closing greater-than symbol. This is because XHTML is based on XML, and the XML rule is that you close empty elements with a slash, like this:

```
<tag/>
```

However, to make this kind of markup readable inside older browsers, you must insert a space before the closing slash, like this:

```
<tag />
```

This space allows older browsers to ignore the closing slash (since they don't know about XHTML). Newer browsers that understand XHTML ignore the space and interpret the tag exactly, which is `<tag/>` (as per the XML rules).

HTML doesn't require a slash with empty elements, but this markup is deprecated (that is, identified as obsolete even though it still occurs in some markup). An HTML empty element looks like this:

```
<tag />
```

Listing 1-1 uses the image element (`<img />`) to include an image on the page:

```
<img src="images/header.gif" alt="header graphic" width="794" height="160" />
```

The `<img />` element references an image. When the browser displays the page, it replaces the `<img />` element with the file that it points to (it uses an attribute to do the pointing, which is shown in the next section). Following the XHTML rule introduced earlier, what appears in HTML as `<img>` appears in XHTML as `<img />` (and this applies to all single tag elements).

You can't make up HTML or XHTML elements. Elements that are legal in (X)HTML are a very specific set — if you use elements that aren't part of the (X)HTML set, every browser ignores them. The elements you can use are defined in the HTML 4.01 or XHTML 1.0 specifications. (The specs for HTML 4.01 can be found at `www.w3.org/TR/html4`, while the specs for XHTML 1.0 can be found at `www.w3.org/TR/xhtml1/`.)

Nesting

Many page structures combine nested elements. Think of your nested elements as *suitcases* that fit neatly inside one another.

For example, a bulleted list uses two kinds of elements:

- The <ul> element specifies that the list is unordered (bulleted).
- The <li> elements mark each item in the list.

When you combine elements by using this method, be sure you close the inside element completely before you close the outside element:

```
<ul>
   <li>Item 1</li>
   <li>Item 2</li>
</ul>
```

Attributes

Attributes allow variety in how an element describes content or works. Attributes let you use elements differently depending on the circumstances. For example, the <img /> element uses the src attribute to specify the location of the image you want to include on your page:

```
<img src="images/header.gif" alt="header graphic" width="794" height="160" />
```

In this bit of HTML, the <img /> element itself is a general flag to the browser that you want to include an image; the src attribute provides the specifics on the image you want to include — header.gif in this instance. Other attributes (such as width and height) provide information about how to display the image, while the alt attribute provides a text alternative to the image that a text-only browser can display (or a text-to-speech reader can say, for the visually impaired).

Chapter 7 describes the <img /> element and its attributes in detail.

You include attributes within the start tag of the element you want them with — after the element name but before the ending sign, like this:

```
<tag attribute="value" attribute="value">
```

XML syntax rules decree that attribute values must always appear in quotation marks, but you can include the attributes and their values in any order within the start tag or within a single tag.

Every (X)HTML element has a collection of attributes that can be used with it, and you can't mix and match attributes and elements. Some attributes can take any text as a value because the value could be anything, like the location of an image or a page you want to link to. Others have a specific list of values the attribute can take, such as your options for aligning text in a table cell.

The HTML 4.01 and XHTML 1.0 specifications define exactly which attributes you can use with any given element and which values (if explicitly defined) each attribute can take.

Each chapter in Parts II and III covers which attributes you can use with each (X)HTML element. Also, see our online content for complete lists of deprecated (X)HTML tags and attributes.

Entities

Text makes the Web possible, but it has limitations. *Entities* are special characters that you can display on your Web page.

Non-ASCII characters

Basic American Standard Code for Information Interchange (ASCII) text defines a fairly small number of characters. It doesn't include some special characters, such as *trademark symbols, fractions,* and *accented characters.*

For example, if we translate a paragraph of text for the page in Figure 1-4 into German, the result includes three *u* characters with umlauts *(ü).*

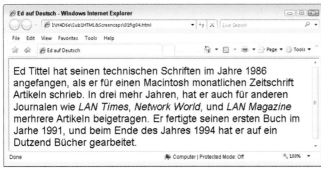

Figure 1-4: ASCII text can't represent all text characters, so HTML entities do instead.

ASCII text doesn't include an umlauted *u,* so HTML uses *entities* to represent such characters. The browser replaces the entity with the character it references. Each entity begins with an ampersand (&) and ends with a semicolon (;); entities come originally from SGML, so we color-code them in purple to reflect their origins. The following markup shows the entities in bold:

```
<html>
<head>
<style>
  body {
    font-family: sans-serif;
    font-size: large;
    }
</style>
<title>Ed auf Deutsch</title>
</head>
<body>
<p>Ed Tittel hat seinen technischen Schriften im Jahre 1986 angefangen, als er
f&uuml;r einen Macintosh monatlichen Zeitschrift Artikeln schrieb. In drei mehr
Jahren, hat er auch f&uuml;r anderen Journalen wie <cite>LAN Times</cite>,
<cite>Network World</cite>, und <cite>LAN Magazine</cite> merhrere Artikeln
beigetragen. Er fertigte seinen ersten Buch im Jarhe 1991, und beim Ende des
Jahres 1994 hat er auf ein Dutzend B&uuml;cher gearbeitet.</p>
</body>
</html>
```

The entity that represents the umlauted *u* is ü.

(X)HTML character codes

The encodings for the ISO-Latin-1 character set are supplied by default, and related entities (a pointer to a complete table appears in Chapter 23) can be invoked and used without special contortions. But using the other encodings mentioned in Table 1-1 requires inclusion of special markup to tell the browser it must be ready to interpret Unicode character codes. (Unicode is an international standard — ISO standard 10646, in fact — that embraces enough character codes to handle most unique alphabets, plus plenty of other symbols and nonalphabetic characters as well.) This special markup takes the form `<meta http-equiv="Content-Type" content="text/html; charset=UTF 8">`; when the value for `charset` is changed to `UTF-8`, you can reference the common Unicode code charts that appear in Chapter 23 of this book.

Tag characters

HTML-savvy software assumes that some HTML characters, such as the greater-than and less-than signs, are meant to be hidden and not displayed on your finished Web page. If you actually want to show a greater-than or less-than sign on your page, you're going to have to make your wishes clear to the browser. The following entities let you display characters that normally are part of the hidden HTML markup:

- **less-than sign (<):** <
- **greater-than sign (>):** >
- **ampersand (&):** &

The < and > signs are used in markup, but these symbols are instructions to the browser and won't show up on the page. If you need these symbols on the Web page, include the entities for them in your markup, like this:

```css
    color: #FFFFFF;
    font-family: Verdana, Arial, Helvetica, sans-serif;
    font-size: 12px;
    }

.bold_text {
    font-weight: bold;
    }

h1 {
    font-family: Verdana, Arial, Helvetica, sans-serif;
    font-weight: bold;
    font-size: 17px;
    color:#96CDFF;
    }

a:link {
    font-weight : bold;
    text-decoration : none;
    color: #FF7A00;
    background: transparent;
    }
a:visited {
    font-weight : bold;
    text-decoration : none;
    color: #91a3b4;
    background: transparent;
    }

a:hover {
    color: #FA0000;
    background: transparent;
    text-decoration : underline;
    }

a:active {
    color: #494949;
    background: transparent;
    font-weight : bold;
    text-decoration : underline;
    }

</style>
</head>

<body>
<table width="794" border="0" align="center" cellpadding="0" cellspacing="0">
  <tr>
    <td>
<!-- Top graphic of Ed and title -->
    <img src="images/header.gif" alt="header graphic" width="794"
    height="160"></td>
  </tr>
  <tr>
```

(continued)

Listing 1-1 *(continued)*

```
<!-- Text about Ed -->
    <td class="white_text"><h1>About me: </h1>
    <p class="white_text">
    Ed Tittel has been working in and around the computer industry since the
    early 1980s, at which point he left academia to work as a programmer. After
    seven years of writing code and managing development projects, he switched
    to the softer side of the industry in pre-sales technical and marketing
    roles. In the period from 1981 to 1994 he worked for 6 companies that
    included Information Research Associates, Burroughs, Schlumberger, and
    Novell.</p>
    <p class="white_text">Ed started writing about computing subjects in 1986
    for a Macintosh oriented monthly magazine. By 1989 he had contributed to
    such publications as LAN Times, Network World, Mac World, and LAN Magazine.
    He worked on his first book in 1991, and by 1994 had contributed to over a
    dozen different titles.</p>
    <p class="white_text">Ed has been freelancing full-time since 1994, with two
    brief stints of other employment interspersed therein (1987-8 at Tivoli,
    <br /> and 2006 at NetQoS, Inc.). He has contributed to over 140 computer
    books, including numerous ...For Dummies titles, college textbooks,
    certification preparation materials, and more. These days, Ed revises an
    occasional book, writes for Tom's Hardware, TechTarget, and Digital Landing,
    and teaches online courses for large corporations including AOL, HP, Sony,
    and Motorola.</p>
    <p class="white_text">To learn more about Ed's professional history, please
    read his <a href="bio.htm">professional bio</a>.</p>
  <h1>Contact:</h1>
    <p class="white_text"><span class="bold_text">Email:</span> etittel at yahoo
    dot com<br />
    <span class="bold_text">Address:</span> 2443 Arbor Drive, Round Rock, TX
    78681-2160<br />
    <span class="bold_text">Phone:</span> 512-252-7497 (No solicitors,
    please)<br />
    <span class="bold_text">List of publications available in:</span>
    <a href="docs/v_et.doc" target="_blank">MS Word</a><br />
    <span class="bold_text">Resume available in:</span>
    <a href="docs/Resu-et13.doc" target="_blank">MS Word</a>
    </p>
    </td>
  </tr>
</table>
</body>
</html>
```

That's a huge amount of HTML to pore over at the very beginning of this
book. Please take our word for it, though: If you read enough of this book's
contents, all of it will make perfect sense!

Chapter 2

Creating and Viewing a Web Page

Creating your very own Web page may seem daunting, but it's definitely fun, and our experience tells us that the best way to get started is to jump right in with both feet. You might splash around a bit at first, but you can keep your head above water without too much thrashing.

This chapter walks you through four basic steps to create a Web page. We don't stop and explain every nuance of the markup you use — we save that for other chapters. Instead, we want to make you comfortable working with markup, and content to create and view a suitably simple Web page.

Before You Get Started

Creating HTML documents differs from creating word-processor documents using an application like Microsoft Word because you end up having to use two applications:

⮑ You create the Web pages in your text or HTML editor.

⮑ You view the results in your Web browser.

Even though many HTML editors, such as Dreamweaver and HTML-Kit, provide a browser preview, it's still important to preview your Web pages inside actual Web browsers (such as Internet Explorer, Firefox, or Safari) so you can see them as your end users do. It might feel a bit unwieldy to edit inside one application and then switch to another to look at your work, but you'll be switching from text editor to browser and back like a pro in (almost) no time.

To get started on your first Web page, you need two types of software:

✔ **A text editor, such as Notepad, TextPad, or SimpleText**

We discuss these tools in more detail in Chapter 22, but here's the thumbnail sketch. Notepad is the native text editor in Windows. TextPad is a shareware text editor available from `www.textpad.com`. SimpleText is the native text editor in the Macintosh operating system.

✔ **A Web browser**

We're going to recommend that you use a plain text editor for your first Web page and here's why:

✔ An advanced HTML editor, such as HotDog Professional or Dreamweaver, often *hides* your HTML from you. For your first page, you want to see your HTML in all of its (limited) glory.

You can make a smooth transition to a more advanced editor after you become familiar with (X)HTML and CSS markup, syntax, and document structure.

✔ Word processors decked out with all the bells and whistles (such as Microsoft Word, in other words) usually insert lots of extra file information behind the scenes (for example, formatting instructions to display or print files). You can't see or change that extra information while you're editing, but what's worse, it interferes with your (X)HTML.

Creating a Page from Scratch

Using HTML to create a Web page from scratch involves four straightforward steps:

1. **Plan your page design.**

2. **Combine HTML and text in a text editor to make that design a reality.**

3. **Save your page.**

4. **View your page in a Web browser.**

So break out your text editor and Web browser — and roll up your sleeves.

Step 1: Planning a simple design

We've discovered that a few minutes spent planning your general approach to a page at the outset of work makes the page-creation process faster and easier.

You don't have to create a complicated diagram or elaborate graphical display in this step. Just jot down some ideas for *what you want on the page* and *how you want it arranged.*

You don't even have to be at your desk to plan a simple design. Take a notepad and pencil outside and design in the sun, or scribble on a napkin while you're having lunch. Remember, this is supposed to be fun.

The example in this chapter is our take on the traditional "Hello World" exercise used in just about every existing programming language: The first thing you learn when tackling a new programming language is how to display the phrase `Hello World` on-screen. In our example, we create a short letter to the world instead, so the page is a bit more substantial and gives you more text to work with. Figure 2-1 shows our basic design for this page.

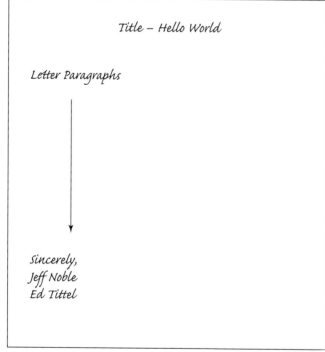

Figure 2-1: Taking a few minutes to sketch your page design makes writing HTML easier.

Title – Hello World

Letter Paragraphs

Sincerely,
Jeff Noble
Ed Tittel

Notes: Teal background
White text

The basic design for the page includes four basic components:

- A serviceable title: "Hello World!"
- A few paragraphs explaining how HTML can help you communicate with the whole world
- A closing of "Sincerely"
- A signature

Jot down some notes about the color scheme you want to use on the page. For our example page we use a teal background and white text, and its title should be "HTML Makes the Web Go Round."

When you know what kind of information you want on the page, you can move on to Step 2 — writing the markup.

Step 2: Writing some HTML

You have a couple of different options when you're ready to create your HTML. In the end, you'll probably use some combination of these:

- If you already have some text that you just want to describe with HTML, save that text as a plain-text file and add HTML markup around it.
- Start creating markup and add the content as you go.

Our example in this chapter starts with some text in Word document format. We saved the content as a text file, opened the text file in our text editor, and added markup around the text.

To save a Word file as a text document, choose File➪Save As. In the dialog box that appears, choose Text Only (*.txt) from the Save As Type drop-down list.

Figure 2-2 shows how our draft letter appears in Microsoft Word before we convert it to text for our page.

Figure 2-2: The letter that is the text for our page, in word-processing form.

Listing 2-1 shows you what you must add to the prose from Microsoft Word to turn it into a fully functional HTML file.

Listing 2-1:   The Complete HTML Page for the 'Hello World!' Letter

```
<!DOCTYPE html PUBLIC "-//W3C//DTD XHTML 1.0 transitional//EN"
        "http://www.w3.org/TR/xhtml1/DTD/xhtml1-transitional.dtd">
<html xmlns="http://www.w3.org/1999/xhtml">

  <head>
    <title>HTML Makes the Web Go Round</title>
  </head>

  <body type="text/css"
        style="color: white;
               background-color: teal;
               font-size: 1.2;
               font-family: sans-serif">

  <h1>Hello World!</h1>

  <p>We sincerely believe that basic HTML knowledge is essential to
     designing, building, and maintaining readable and workable Web
     pages. Our goal in this book is to explain what HTML, XHTML, and
     CSS are and how they work, and then to show you exactly how to
     use them to best advantage.
  </p>

  <p>Along the way, we will examine the principles and best practices
     that govern Web page design and construction, and help you
     understand how to make your content accessible to the broadest
     possible audience.
  </p>

  <p>By the time you work your way through this book's contents, you
     should feel comfortable with creating and managing your own Web
     site. You should also understand what it takes to identify your
     audience, communicate with that audience, and keep your content
     fresh and interesting to keep them coming back for more.
  </p>

  <p>Sincerely,<br />
     Jeff Noble and Ed Tittel, your humble authors
  </p>

  </body>
</html>
```

The HTML markup includes a collection of markup elements and attributes that describe the letter's contents:

- ✔ The <html> element defines the document as an HTML document.
- ✔ The <head> element creates a header section for the document.
- ✔ The <title> element defines a document title that is displayed in the browser's title bar.

  The <title> element is *inside* the <head> element.

- ✔ The <body> element holds the text that appears in the browser window.

  The markup that follows the style=" " attribute inside the <body> element is CSS, otherwise known as the *C*ascading *S*tyle *S*heet markup language. It says we want white text on a teal background, where the text is larger than usual, and in a sans-serif font. (You'll find out all about styles and attributes in Chapters 8 and 9.)

- ✔ The <h1> element marks the Hello World text as a first-level heading.
- ✔ The <p> elements identify each paragraph of the document.
- ✔ The <br /> element adds a manual line break after Sincerely.

Don't worry about the ins and outs of how the HTML elements work. They are covered in detail in Chapters 4 and 5. Also, please note that a Web page can include graphics, scripts, and other elements that we deliberately avoid in this contrived and simple example to keep things . . . well . . . simple! We will cover all these extras in profuse detail later in the book, though.

After you create a complete HTML page (or the first chunk of it that you want to review), you must save it before you can see your work in a browser.

Step 3: Saving your page

You use a text editor to create HTML documents and a Web browser to view them, but before you can let your browser loose on your HTML page, you must save that page. When you're just building a page, you should save a copy of it to your local hard drive and view it locally with your browser.

Choosing a location and name for your file

When you save your file to your hard drive, keep the following in mind:

- ✔ You need to be able to find it again.

  Create a folder on your hard drive especially for your Web pages. Call it Web Pages or HTML (or any other name that makes sense to you), and be sure to put it somewhere easy to find.

✔ The name should make sense to you so you can identify file contents without actually opening the file.

✔ The name should work well in a Web browser.

Don't use spaces in the name. Some operating systems — most notably Unix and Linux (the most popular Web-hosting operating systems around) — don't tolerate spaces in filenames; use an underscore (_) or hyphen (-) instead. It's also a good idea to avoid other punctuation characters in filenames, and in general, to keep them as short as you can.

In our example, we saved our file in a folder called Web Pages and named it (drum roll, please) html_letter.html, as shown in Figure 2-3.

Figure 2-3:
Use a handy
location and
a logical
filename
for HTML
pages.

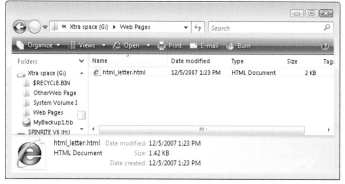

Figure 2-3:
Use a handy
location and
a logical
filename
for HTML
pages.

.htm or .html

You can actually choose from one of two suffixes for your pages: .html or .htm. (Our example filename, html_letter.html, uses the .html suffix.)

The shorter .htm is a relic from the "8.3" DOS days when filenames could only include eight characters plus a three-character suffix that described the file's type. Today, operating systems can support long filenames and suffixes that are longer than three letters, so we suggest you stick with .html.

Web servers and Web browsers handle both .htm and .html equally well.

Stick with one filename option. .html and .htm files are treated the same by browsers and servers, but they're actually different suffixes, so they create different filenames. (The name html_letter.html is different from html_letter.htm.) This difference matters a lot when you create hyperlinks (covered in Chapter 6).

Step 4: Viewing your page

After you save a copy of your page, you're ready to view it in a Web browser. Follow these steps to view your Web page in Internet Explorer. (Steps may be different if you're using a different browser.)

1. **If you haven't opened your browser, do that now.**

2. **Choose File⇨Open.**

3. **In the Open dialog box that appears, click the Browse button.**

4. **In the new dialog that appears, navigate your file system until you find your HTML file, and then select it so it appears in the File name area.**

   Figure 2-4 shows a highlighted HTML file, ready to be opened.

Figure 2-4: Use Internet Explorer to navigate to your Web pages.

5. **Click the Open button,**

   You are brought back to the Open dialog box. (***Note:*** Newer versions of IE will warn you they must open a new browser window for your local file, for security reasons, if you're already connected to the Internet; this is perfectly OK.)

6. **Click OK.**

   The page appears in your Web browser in all its glory, as shown in Figure 2-5.

Part II

Formatting Web Pages with (X)HTML

The 5th Wave   By Rich Tennant

©RICHTENNANT

Well, there's your Web page, Crypto. Designed like you asked. But personally, I think it has too many spinning spirals and blinking lights. It makes...hard reading. Make...tired... look...at...lose...all... con...cen...tra...tion...

Perfect!

CRYPTO THE HYPNOTIST

In this part . . .

*I*n this part of the book, we describe the markup and document structures that make Web pages workable and attractive. To begin with, we examine gross HTML document structure, including document headers and bodies, and how to put the right pieces together. After that, we talk about organizing text in blocks and lists. Next, we explain how linking works in (X)HTML and how it provides the glue that ties the entire World Wide Web together. To wrap things up, we also explain how to add graphics to your pages. Thus, we cover the basic building blocks for well-constructed, properly proportioned Web pages — and not by coincidence, either

Chapter 4

Creating (X)HTML Document Structure

. . . .

In This Chapter

▷ Creating a basic (X)HTML document structure

▷ Defining the (X)HTML document header

▷ Creating a full-bodied (X)HTML document

. . . .

*T*he framework for a simple (X)HTML document consists of a head and body. The head provides information about the document to the browser, and the body contains information that appears in the browser window. The first step toward creating any (X)HTML document is defining its framework.

This chapter covers the major elements needed to set up the basic structure of an (X)HTML document — including its head and body. We also show you how to tell the browser which version of HTML or XHTML you're using. Although version information isn't necessary for users, browsers use it to make sure they display document content correctly for your users.

Establishing a Document Structure

Although no two (X)HTML pages are alike — each employs a unique combination of content and elements to define a page — every properly constructed (X)HTML page follows the same basic document structure:

   ✔ A statement that identifies the document as an (X)HTML document

   ✔ A document header

   ✔ A document body

Each time you create an (X)HTML document, you start with these three elements; then you fill in the rest of your content and markup to create an individual page.

Although a basic document structure is a requirement for every (X)HTML document, creating it over and over again gets a little monotonous. Most (X)HTML-editing tools set up basic document structure automatically whenever you open a new document.

Labeling Your (X)HTML Document

At the top of your (X)HTML document sits the *Document Type Declaration,* or `DOCTYPE` *declaration.* This line of code specifies which version of HTML or XHTML you're using, and in turn lets browsers know how to interpret the document. We use the XHTML 1.0 specification in this chapter because it's widely used, and what most browsers and editing tools expect to see.

Adding an HTML DOCTYPE declaration

If you choose to create an HTML 4.01 document instead of an XHTML document, you can pick from three possible `DOCTYPE` declarations:

- **HTML 4.01 Transitional:** This is the most inclusive version of HTML 4.01, and it incorporates all HTML structural elements, as well as all presentation elements:

  ```
  <!DOCTYPE HTML PUBLIC "-//W3C//DTD HTML 4.01 Transitional//EN"
          "http://www.w3.org/TR/html4/loose.dtd">
  ```

- **HTML 4.01 Strict:** This streamlined version of HTML excludes all presentation-related elements in favor of style sheets as a mechanism for driving display:

  ```
  <!DOCTYPE HTML PUBLIC "-//W3C//DTD HTML 4.01//EN"
          "http://www.w3.org/TR/html4/strict.dtd">
  ```

- **HTML 4.01 Frameset:** This version begins with HTML 4.01 Transitional and adds all the elements that make frames possible:

  ```
  <!DOCTYPE HTML PUBLIC "-//W3C//DTD HTML 4.01 Frameset//EN"
          "http://www.w3.org/TR/html4/frameset.dtd">
  ```

Adding an XHTML DOCTYPE declaration

To create an XHTML document, use one of the following `DOCTYPE` declarations:

✔ **XHTML 1.0 Transitional:**

```
<!DOCTYPE html PUBLIC "-//W3C//DTD XHTML 1.0 Transitional//EN"
        "http://www.w3.org/TR/xhtml1/DTD/xhtml1-transitional.dtd">
```

✔ **XHTML 1.0 Strict:**

```
<!DOCTYPE html "-//W3C//DTD XHTML 1.0 Strict//EN"
        "http://www.w3.org/TR/xhtml1/DTD/xhtml1-strict.dtd">
```

✔ **XHTML 1.0 Frameset:**

```
<!DOCTYPE html PUBLIC "-//W3C//DTD XHTML 1.0 Frameset//EN"
        "http://www.w3.org/TR/xhtml1/DTD/xhtml1-frameset.dtd">
```

The XHTML DTD descriptions are similar to the HTML DTD descriptions defined in Chapter 1.

The <html> element

After you specify which version of (X)HTML the document follows, add an <html> element to contain all other (X)HTML elements in your page:

```
<!DOCTYPE html PUBLIC "-//W3C//DTD XHTML 1.0 Transitional//EN"
        "http://www.w3.org/TR/xhtml1/DTD/xhtml1-transitional.dtd">

<html>



</html>
```

Adding the XHTML namespace

A *namespace* is a collection of names used by the elements and attributes in an XML document. XHTML uses a special collection of names; therefore it needs a namespace that looks like this:

```
<!DOCTYPE html PUBLIC "-//W3C//DTD XHTML 1.0 Transitional//EN"
        "http://www.w3.org/TR/xhtml1/DTD/xhtml1-transitional.dtd">

<html xmlns="http://www.w3.org/1999/xhtml">



</html>
```

Don't get bogged down by the meaning of namespaces. If you work with other XML vocabularies, you need to know about namespaces. For simple XHTML documents, you just need to remember to include the XHTML namespace. The preceding code snippet shows you exactly how to do so!

Adding a Document Header

The *head* of an (X)HTML document is one of two main components in a document. (The *body* of the document is the other main component.) The head, or *header,* provides basic information *about* the document, including its title and metadata (or information about information), such as keywords, author information, and a description. If you wish to use a style sheet with your page, you also include information about that style sheet in the header.

Chapter 8 provides a complete overview of creating Cascading Style Sheets (CSS) and shows you how to include them in (X)HTML documents.

The `<head>` element, which defines the page header, immediately follows the `<html>` opening tag:

```
<!DOCTYPE html PUBLIC "-//W3C//DTD XHTML 1.0 Transitional//EN"
        "http://www.w3.org/TR/xhtml1/DTD/xhtml1-transitional.dtd">

<html xmlns="http://www.w3.org/1999/xhtml">
  <head>

  </head>
</html>
```

Giving your page a title

Every (X)HTML page needs a descriptive title to tell visitors what the page is about. This text appears in the title bar at the very top of the browser window, as shown in Figure 4-1. A page title should be concise yet informative. (For example, *My home page* isn't as informative as *Jeff's Web Design Services.*)

Define a page title by using the `<title>` element inside the `<head>` element:

```
<!DOCTYPE html PUBLIC "-//W3C//DTD XHTML 1.0 Transitional//EN"
        "http://www.w3.org/TR/xhtml1/DTD/xhtml1-transitional.dtd">

<html xmlns="http://www.w3.org/1999/xhtml">
  <head>
    <title>Jeff's Web Design Services</title>
  </head>

</html>
```

Figure 4-1:
(X)HTML
page titles
appear in a
Web brows-
er's window
title bar.

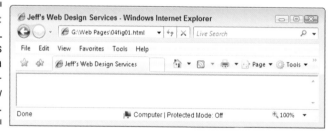

Search engines use `<title>` contents when they list Web pages in response to a query. The page title may be the first thing a Web surfer reads about your page, especially if she finds it using a search engine. In fact, a search engine will probably list your page title with many others on a search results page, which gives you only one chance to grab the Web surfer's attention and convince her to choose your page. A well-crafted title can do just that.

The title is also used for Bookmarks and in a browser's History; therefore keep your titles short and sweet.

Defining metadata

The term *metadata* refers to data about data. In the context of the Web, that means data that describes your Web page. Metadata for a page may include

- Keywords
- A description of your page
- Information about the page author
- The software application you used to create the page

Elements and attributes

You define each piece of metadata for your (X)HTML page with

- The `<meta />` element
- The `name` and `content` attributes

For example, the following elements create a list of keywords and a description for a consulting-service page:

```
<!DOCTYPE html PUBLIC "-//W3C//DTD XHTML 1.0 Transitional//EN"
         "http://www.w3.org/TR/xhtml1/DTD/xhtml1-transitional.dtd">

<html xmlns="http://www.w3.org/1999/xhtml">
  <head>
  <title>Jeff's Web Design Services</title>
  <meta name="keywords"
        content="Web consulting, page design, site construction" />
  <meta name="description"
        content="Synopsis of Jeff's skills and services" />
  </head>
</html>
```

Custom names

The (X)HTML specification doesn't

✔ Predefine the kinds of metadata you can include in your page

✔ Specify how to name different pieces of metadata, such as keywords and descriptions

So (for example) instead of using `keywords` and `description` as names for keyword and description metadata, you can just as easily use `kwrd` and `desc`, as in the following markup:

```
<!DOCTYPE html PUBLIC "-//W3C//DTD XHTML 1.0 Transitional//EN"
         "http://www.w3.org/TR/xhtml1/DTD/xhtml1-transitional.dtd">

<html xmlns="http://www.w3.org/1999/xhtml">
  <head>
    <title>Jeff's Web Design Services</title>
    <meta name="kwrd"
          content=" Web consulting, page design, site construction " />
    <meta name="desc" content="Synopsis of Jeff's skills and services" />
  </head>
</html>
```

If you can use just any old values for the `<meta>` element's `name` and `content` attributes, how do systems know what to do with your metadata? The answer is — they don't. Each search engine works differently. Although keywords and description are commonly used metadata names, many search engines may not recognize or use other metadata elements that you include.

Many developers use metadata to either

✔ Leave messages for others who may look at the source code of the page

✔ Prepare for future browsers and search engines that use the metadata

Chapter 5

Text and Lists

*H*TML documents consist of text, images, multimedia files, links, and other bits of content that you meld together into a page by using markup elements and attributes. You use blocks of text to create such things as headings, paragraphs, and lists. The first step in creating a solid HTML document is laying a firm foundation that establishes the document's structure.

Formatting Text

Here's a plus-ultra-technical definition of a *block of text:* some chunk of content that wraps from one line to another inside an HTML element.

In fact, your HTML page is a giant collection of blocks of text:

▱ Every bit of content on your page must be part of some block element.

▱ Every block element sits within the `<body>` element on your page.

HTML recognizes several kinds of text blocks that you can use in your document, including (but not limited to)

▱ Paragraphs

▱ Headings

▱ Block quotes

▱ Lists

▱ Tables

▱ Forms

Inline elements versus text blocks

The difference between inline elements and a block of text is important. HTML elements in this chapter describe blocks of text. An *inline element* is a word or string of words *inside* a block element (for example, text emphasis elements such as `<em>` or `<strong>`). Inline elements must be nested within a block element; otherwise, your HTML document isn't syntactically correct.

Inline elements, such as linking and formatting elements, are designed to link from (or change the appearance of) a few words or lines of content found inside those blocks.

Paragraphs

Paragraphs appear more often in Web pages than any other kind of text block.

HTML browsers don't recognize hard returns that you enter when you create your page inside an editor. You must use a `<p>` element to tell the browser to separate all contained text up to the closing `</p>` as a paragraph.

Formatting

To create a paragraph, follow these steps:

1. **Add** `<p>` **in the body of the document.**

2. **Type the content of the paragraph.**

3. **Add** `</p>` **to close that paragraph.**

Here's what it looks like:

```
<!DOCTYPE html PUBLIC "-//W3C//DTD XHTML 1.0 Transitional//EN"
        "http://www.w3.org/TR/xhtml1/DTD/xhtml1-transitional.dtd">
<html xmlns="http://www.w3.org/1999/xhtml">
  <head>
    <meta http-equiv="Content-Type" content="text/html; charset=ISO-8859-1" />
    <title>All About Blocks</title>
  </head>

  <body>
    <p>This is a paragraph. It's a very simple structure that you will use
       time and again in your Web pages.</p>
    <p><b>This</b> is another paragraph. What could be simpler to create?</p>
  </body>
</html>
```

This HTML page includes two paragraphs, each marked with a separate <p> element. Most Web browsers add a line break and a full line of white space after every paragraph on your page, as shown in Figure 5-1.

Figure 5-1:
Web browsers delineate paragraphs with line breaks.

Sloppy HTML coders don't use the closing </p> tag when they create paragraphs. Although some browsers permit this dubious practice without yelling, omitting the closing tag

- Isn't correct syntax
- Causes problems with style sheets
- Can cause a page to appear inconsistently from one browser to another

You can control paragraph formatting (color, style, size, and alignment) by using Cascading Style Sheets (CSS), which we cover in Chapters 8 and 9.

Alignment

By default, the paragraph aligns to the left. You can use the align attribute with a value of left, center, right, or justify to control its alignment explicitly.

```
<p align="center">This paragraph is centered.</p>
<p align="right">This paragraph is right-justified.</p>
<p align="justify">This paragraph is left- and right-justified; to show
    this effect at work, we need several lines of text. Notice that
    both right and left margins end up flush when you use this particular
    value for the align attribute. In particular, the second and third
    lines of text show extra space between the words.</p>
```

Figure 5-2 shows how a Web browser aligns each paragraph according to the value of the align attribute.

The align attribute has been deprecated (made obsolete) in favor of using CSS (see Chapter 8).

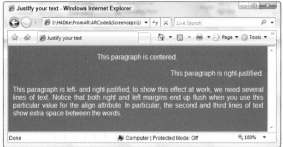

Figure 5-2: Use the `align` attribute with a paragraph to specify horizontal alignment.

Headings

Headings break a document into sections. This book uses headings and sub-headings to divide every chapter into sections, and you can do the same with your Web page. Headings

- Create an organizational structure
- Break up the visual appearance of the page
- Give visual clues about how pieces of content are grouped

HTML includes six elements for up to six different heading levels in your documents:

- `<h1>` is the most prominent heading (Heading 1)
- `<h6>` is the least prominent heading (Heading 6)

Follow order from highest to lowest as you use HTML heading levels. That is, don't use a second-level heading until you've used a first-level heading, don't use a third-level heading until you've used a second, and so on. If you want to change how headings look, Chapter 8 and Chapter 9 show you how to use style sheets for that purpose.

Formatting

To create a heading, follow these steps:

1. **Add** `<h`*n*`>` **in the body of your document.**

2. **Type the content for the heading.**

3. **Add** `</h`*n*`>`.

Browser displays

Every browser has a different way of displaying heading levels, as you see in the next two sections.

Graphical browsers

Most graphical browsers use a distinctive size and typeface for headings:

- First-level headings (`<h1>`) are the largest (usually two or three font sizes larger than the default text size for paragraphs).

- All headings use boldface type by default, whereas paragraph text uses plain (non-bold) type by default.

- Sixth-level headings (`<h6>`) are the smallest and may be two or three font sizes *smaller* than the default paragraph text.

The following snippet of HTML markup shows all six headings at work:

```
<!DOCTYPE html PUBLIC "-//W3C//DTD XHTML 1.0 Transitional//EN"
        "http://www.w3.org/TR/xhtml1/DTD/xhtml1-transitional.dtd">
<html xmlns="http://www.w3.org/1999/xhtml">
  <head>
    <meta http-equiv="Content-Type" content="text/html; charset=ISO-8859-1" />
    <title>All About Blocks</title>
  </head>

  <body>
    <h1>First-level heading</h1>
    <h2>Second-level heading</h2>
    <h3>Third-level heading</h3>
    <h4>Fourth-level heading</h4>
    <h5>Fifth-level heading</h5>
    <h6>Sixth-level heading</h6>
  </body>
</html>
```

Figure 5-3 shows this HTML page as rendered in a browser.

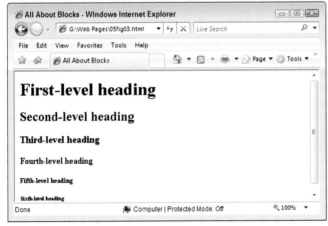

Figure 5-3: Web browsers display headings in decreasing size from level one to level six.

Use CSS to control the display of headings, including color, size, spacing, and alignment.

By default, most browsers use Times Roman fonts for headings. The font size decreases as heading level increases. (Default sizes for first- through sixth-level headings are, respectively, 24, 18, 14, 12, 10, and 8.) You can override any of this formatting by using CSS.

Text browsers

Text-only browsers use heading conventions different from those of graphical browsers because text-only browsers use a single character size and font to display all content.

Controlling Text Blocks

Blocks of text build the foundation for your page. You can break those blocks into smaller pieces to better guide readers through your content.

Block quotes

A *block quote* is a long quotation or excerpt from a printed source that you set apart on your page. Use the `<blockquote>` element to identify block quotes:

```
<!DOCTYPE html PUBLIC "-//W3C//DTD XHTML 1.0 Transitional//EN"
        "http://www.w3.org/TR/xhtml1/DTD/xhtml1-transitional.dtd">
<html xmlns="http://www.w3.org/1999/xhtml">
  <head>
    <meta http-equiv="Content-Type" content="text/html; charset=ISO-8859-1" />
    <title>Famous Quotations</title>
  </head>

  <body>
    <h1>An Inspiring Quote</h1>
    <p>When I need a little inspiration to remind me of why I spend my days
       in the classroom, I just remember what Lee Iococca said:</p>
    <blockquote>
      In a completely rational society, the best of us would be teachers
      and the rest of us would have to settle for something else.
    </blockquote>
  </body>
</html>
```

Most Web browsers display block-quote content with a slight left indent, as shown in Figure 5-4.

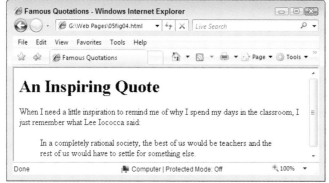

Figure 5-4:
Web
browsers
typically
indent a
block quote
to separate
it from
paragraphs.

Preformatted text

Ordinarily, HTML ignores white space inside documents. A browser won't display a block element's

- ✔ Hard returns
- ✔ Line breaks
- ✔ Large white spaces

The following markup includes several hard returns, line breaks, and a lot of space characters. Figure 5-5 shows that the Web browser ignores all of this.

```
<p>This is a paragraph

    with a lot of white space

        thrown in for fun (and as a test of course).</p>
```

Figure 5-5:
Web
browsers
routinely
ignore white
space.

The preformatted text element (`<pre>`) instructs browsers to keep all white space intact as it displays your content (like the following sample). Use the `<pre>` element in place of the `<p>` element to make the browser apply all your white space, as shown in Figure 5-6.

```
<!DOCTYPE html PUBLIC "-//W3C//DTD XHTML 1.0 Transitional//EN"
        "http://www.w3.org/TR/xhtml1/DTD/xhtml1-transitional.dtd">
<html xmlns="http://www.w3.org/1999/xhtml">
  <head>
    <meta http-equiv="Content-Type" content="text/html; charset=ISO-8859-1" />
    <title>White space</title>
  </head>

  <body>
    <pre>This is a paragraph

      with a lot of white space

      thrown in for fun (and as a test of course).
    </pre>
  </body>
</html>
```

Figure 5-6: Use preformatted text to force browsers to recognize white space.

You may want the browser to display white spaces in an HTML page where proper spacing is important, such as for

✔ Code samples

✔ Text tables

You can nest `<pre>` elements inside `<blockquote>` elements to carefully control how lines of quoted text appear on the page. Or better still, forget about these tags and use CSS to position text blocks inside `<div>` elements.

Use CSS if you want more control over the formatting of your lists, including the ability to use your own graphics as bullet symbols.

Definition lists

Definition lists group terms and definitions into a single list and require three different elements to complete the list:

- ✔ <dl>: Holds the list definitions.
- ✔ <dt>: Defines a term in the list.
- ✔ <dd>: Defines a definition for a term.

You can have as many terms (defined by <dt>) in a list as you need. Each term can have one or more definitions (defined by <dd>).

To create a definition list with two items requires elements and content in the following order:

1. <dl>
2. <dt>
3. First term name
4. </dt>
5. <dd>
6. Content for the definition of the first item
7. </dd>
8. <dt>
9. Second term name
10. </dt>
11. <dd>
12. Content for the definition of the second item
13. </dd>
14. </dl>

The following definition list includes three terms, one of which has two definitions:

```
<!DOCTYPE html PUBLIC "-//W3C//DTD XHTML 1.0 Transitional//EN"
        "http://www.w3.org/TR/xhtml1/DTD/xhtml1-transitional.dtd">
<html xmlns="http://www.w3.org/1999/xhtml">
  <head>
```

```
    <meta http-equiv="Content-Type" content="text/html; charset=ISO-8859-1" />
    <title>Definition Lists</title>
  </head>

  <body>
    <h1>Markup Language Definitions</h1>
    <dl>
      <dt>SGML</dt>
        <dd>The Standard Generalized Markup Language</dd>
      <dt>HTML</dt>
        <dd>The Hypertext Markup Language</dd>
        <dd>The markup language you use to create Web pages.</dd>
      <dt>XML</dt>
        <dd>The Extensible Markup Language</dd>
    </dl>
  </body>
</html>
```

Figure 5-16 shows how a browser displays this HTML.

Figure 5-16:
Definition lists group terms and their related definitions into one list.

If you think the items in a list are too close together, you can take one of two actions:

↙ Put two `<br/>` elements before each `</li>` or `</dd>` element to add more white space.

↙ Use CSS styles to carefully control all aspects of list appearance, as shown in Chapter 8.

Note that definition lists often display differently inside different browsers, and aren't always handled the same by search engines or text-to-speech translators. Alas, this means definition lists may not be the best choice of formatting for lists you create (even lists of definitions). See the excellent coverage of this topic at www.maxdesign.com/au/presentation/ definition for a more detailed discussion.

Nesting lists

You can create subcategories by *nesting* lists within lists. Some common uses for nested lists include

- Site maps and other navigation tools
- Tables of contents for online books and papers
- Outlines

You can combine any of the three kinds of lists to create *nested lists,* such as a multilevel table of contents or an outline that mixes numbered headings with bulleted list items as the lowest outline level.

The following example starts with a numbered list that defines a list of things to do for the day, and uses three bulleted lists to break down those items further, into specific tasks:

```
<!DOCTYPE html PUBLIC "-//W3C//DTD XHTML 1.0 Transitional//EN"
        "http://www.w3.org/TR/xhtml1/DTD/xhtml1-transitional.dtd">
<html xmlns="http://www.w3.org/1999/xhtml">
  <head>
    <meta http-equiv="Content-Type" content="text/html; charset=ISO-8859-1" />
    <title>Nested Lists</title>
  </head>

  <body>
    <h1>Things to do today</h1>
    <ol>
      <li>Feed cat</li>
        <ul>
          <li>Rinse bowl</li>
          <li>Open cat food</li>
          <li>Mix dry and wet food in bowl</li>
          <li>Deliver on a silver platter to Fluffy</li>
        </ul>
      <li>Wash car</li>
        <ul>
          <li>Vacuum interior</li>
          <li>Wash exterior</li>
          <li>Wax exterior</li>
        </ul>
      <li>Grocery shopping</li>
        <ul>
          <li>Plan meals</li>
```

```
            <li>Clean out fridge</li>
            <li>Make list</li>
            <li>Go to store</li>
          </ul>
        </ol>
      </body>
    </html>
```

All nested lists follow the same markup pattern:

✔ Each list item in the top-level ordered list is followed by a complete second-level list.

✔ The second-level lists sit inside the top-level list, not in the list items.

Figure 5-17 shows how a browser reflects this nesting in its display.

Figure 5-17: Nested lists combine lists for a multilevel organization of information.

As you build nested lists, watch opening and closing tags carefully. Close first what you opened last is an important axiom. If you don't open and close tags properly, lists might not use consistent indents or numbers, or text might be indented incorrectly because a list somewhere was never properly closed.

Chapter 6

Linking to Online Resources

*H*yperlinks, or simply *links,* connect (X)HTML pages and other resources on the Web. When you include a link on your page, you enable visitors to travel from your page to another Web site, another page on your site, or even another location on the same page. Without links, a page stands alone, disconnected from the rest of the Web. With links, that page becomes part of an almost boundless collection of information.

Basic Links

To create a link, you need

▶ **The Web address** (called a Uniform Resource Locator, or URL) for the Web site or file that's your link target. This usually starts with `http://`.

▶ **Some text** in your Web page to label or describe the link.

Try to ensure that the text you use says something useful about the resource being linked.

▶ **An anchor element (`<a>`) with `href` attribute** to bring it all together.

The element to create links is called an *anchor element* because you use it to anchor a URL to some text on your page. When users view your page in a browser, they can click the text to activate the link and visit the page whose URL you specified in that link. You insert the full URL in the `href` attribute. This tells the link where to go.

You can think of the structure of a basic link as a cheeseburger (or your preferred vegan substitute). The URL is the cheese, the patty is the link text, and the anchor tags are the buns. Tasty, yes?

For example, if you have a Web page that describes HTML standards, you may want to refer Web surfers to the World Wide Web Consortium (W3C) — the organization that governs all things related to (X)HTML standards. A basic link to the W3C's Web site, `www.w3.org`, looks like this:

```
<p>The <a href="http://www.w3.org">World Wide Web Consortium</a> is the
   standards body that oversees the ongoing development of the XHTML
   specification.</p>
```

You specify the link URL (`http://www.w3.org`) in the anchor element's `href` attribute. The text (`World Wide Web Consortium`) between the anchor element's open and close tags (`<a>` and `</a>`) labels or describes the link.

Figure 6-1 shows how a browser displays this bit of markup.

Figure 6-1:
A paragraph
with a link to
the W3C.

You can also anchor URLs to images so users can click an image to activate a link. (For more about creating images that link, see Chapter 7.)

For a detailed discussion of the ins and outs of URLs, see Chapter 1.

Link options

You can link to a variety of online resources:

- Other (X)HTML pages (either on your Web site or on another Web site)
- Different locations on the same (X)HTML page
- Resources that aren't even (X)HTML pages at all, such as e-mail addresses, pictures, and text files

Anchor elements aren't block elements

Anchor elements are *inline elements* — they apply to a few words or characters within a block of text (the text that you want to use as a link) instead of defining formatting for blocks of text. The anchor element typically sits inside a paragraph (<p>) or other block element, such as a paragraph or list item. When you create a link, you should always create it within a block element, such as a paragraph, list item, heading, or even a table cell. Turn to Chapter 5 for more information on block elements.

Although many Web browsers display anchors just fine even if you don't nest them in block elements, some browsers don't handle this breach of (X)HTML syntax very well — these, for example:

- Text-only browsers for Palm devices and mobile phones

- Text-to-speech readers for the visually impaired

Text-based browsers rely on block elements to properly divide the sections of your page. Without a block element, these browsers might display your links in the wrong places.

Link locations, captions, and destinations have a big impact on how site visitors perceive links. Chapter 3 covers best practices for using links in your site design.

The kind of link you create is determined by where you link.

Absolute links

An *absolute link* uses a complete URL to connect browsers to a Web page or online resource.

Links that use a complete URL to point to a resource are called *absolute* because they provide a complete, stand-alone path to another Web resource. When you link to a page on someone else's Web site, the Web browser needs every bit of information in the URL to find the page. The browser starts with the domain in the URL and works its way through the path to a specific file.

When you link to files on someone else's site, you must always use absolute URLs in the `href` attribute of the anchor element. Here's an example:

```
http://www.website.com/directory/page.html
```

Relative links

A *relative link* uses a kind of shorthand to specify the URL for the resource where you're pointing.

Use the following guidelines with relative links in your (X)HTML pages:

- ✔ You create relative links between resources in the same domain.

- ✔ Because both resources are in the same domain, you can omit domain information from the URL.

  A *relative* URL uses the location of the resource you're linking from to identify the location of the resource you're linking to (for example, `page.html`).

A relative link is similar to telling someone that he or she needs to go to the Eastside Mall. If the person already knows where the Eastside Mall is, he or she doesn't need additional directions. Web browsers behave the same way.

If you use relative links on your site, your links still work if you change either

- ✔ Servers

- ✔ Domain names

Simple links

You can take advantage of relative URLs when you create a link between pages on the same Web site. If you want to make a link from `http://www.mysite.com/home.html` to `http://www.mysite.com/about.html`, you can use this simplified, relative URL in an anchor element on `home.html`:

```
<p>Learn more <a href="about.html">about</a> our company.</p>
```

When a browser sees a link without a domain name, the browser assumes the link is *relative* — and uses the domain and path from the linking page to find the linked page.

Site links

As your site grows more complex and you organize your files into various folders, you can still use relative links. But you must provide additional information in the URL to help the browser find files that don't reside in the same directory as the file from which you're linking.

Use `../` (two periods and a slash) before the filename to indicate that the browser should move up one level in the directory structure.

The markup for this process looks like this:

```
<a href="../docs/home.html>Documentation home</a>
```

The notation in this anchor element instructs the browser to:

1. **Move up one folder from the folder the linking document is stored in.**

2. **Find a folder called** `docs`.

3. **Find a file called** `home.html`.

When you create a relative link, the location of the file *to* which you link is always relative to the file *from* which you link. As you create a relative URL, trace the path a browser takes if it starts on the page you're linking from to get to the page to which you're linking. That path defines the URL you need.

Common mistakes

Every Web resource — whether it's a site, page, or image — has a unique URL. Even one incorrect letter in your URL can lead to a *broken link*. Broken links lead

to an error page (often the HTTP error `404 File or directory not found`).

URLs are so finicky that a simple typo breaks a link.

If a URL doesn't work, try these tactics:

✔ **Check the capitalization.** Some Web servers (Linux and UNIX most notably) are *case-sensitive* (meaning they distinguish between capital and lowercase letters). These servers treat the filenames `Bios.html` and `bios.html` as different files on the Web server. That means any browser looking for a particular URL *must* use uppercase and lowercase letters when necessary. Be sure the capitalization in the link matches the capitalization of the URL.

To avoid problems with files on your Web site, follow a standard naming convention. Often, using only lowercase letters can simplify your life.

✔ **Check the extension.** `Bios.htm` and `Bios.html` are two different files. If your link's URL uses one extension and the actual filename uses another, your link won't work.

To avoid problems with extensions on your Web site, pick either `.html` or `.htm` *and stick to that extension.*

✔ **Check the filename.** `bio.html` and `bios.html` are two different files.

✔ **Cut and paste.** Avoid retyping a URL if you can copy it. The best and most foolproof way to create a URL that works is as follows:

1. **Load a page in your browser.**

2. **Copy the URL from the browser's address or link text box.**

3. **Paste the URL into your (X)HTML markup.**

The importance of http:// in (X)HTML links

Browsers make surfing the Web as easy as possible. If you type **www.sun.com**, **sun. com**, or often even just **sun**, in your browser's address window, the browser obligingly brings up `http://www.sun.com`. Although this technique works when you type URLs into your browser window, it doesn't work when you're writing markup.

The URLs that you use in your HTML markup must be fully formed. Browsers won't interpret URLs that don't include the page protocol. If you forget the `http://`, your link may not work!

The cut and paste method for grabbing URLs presumes you're grabbing them from a Web site somewhere. If you open a local file on your PC in a browser, you'll see something that looks like this: `file:\\\I:\H4D6e\html_ letter.html`. The `file:\\\` is an Internet Explorer convention used to identify the document as a file in your local file system, `I:\` is a drive letter, the `H4D6e\` is a folder or directory on that drive, and the rightmost text element (`html_letter.html` in this case) is the name of the HTML file you've opened. You can't use URLs like this on a Web site, so please — don't try to!

Customizing Links

You can customize links to

- Open linked documents in new windows
- Link to specific locations *within* a Web page of your own
- Link to items other than (X)HTML pages, such as
  - Portable Document Format (PDF) files
  - Compressed files
  - Word-processing documents

New windows

The Web works because you can link pages on your Web site to pages on other people's Web sites by using a simple anchor element. But when you link to someone else's site, you send users away from your own site.

To keep users on your site, HTML can open the linked page in a new window. The simple addition of the `target` attribute to an anchor element opens that link in a new browser window instead of opening it in the current window:

```
<p>The <a href="http://www.w3.org" target="_blank">World Wide Web Consortium</a>
is the standards body that oversees the ongoing development of the XHTML
specification.</p>
```

When you give a `target` attribute a `_blank` value, this tells the browser to

1. **Keep the linking page open in the current window.**
2. **Open the linked page in a new window.**

The result of the `target="_blank"` attribute is shown in Figure 6-2.

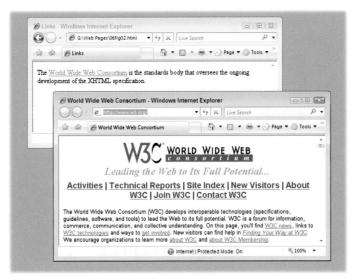

Figure 6-2:
Use the
target
attribute to
open a new
window for
a linked file.

Pop-up windows irritate some users.

You can use JavaScript to control the size, location, and appearance of pop-up windows, as well as put buttons on them to help users close them quickly. Chapter 12 covers pop-up windows in more detail — including JavaScript details.

Locations in Web pages

Locations within Web pages can be marked for direct access by links on

- The same page
- The same Web site
- Other Web sites

Keep these considerations in mind when adding links to Web pages:

- Several short pages may present information more conveniently for readers than one long page with internal links.

  Links within large pages work nicely for quick access to directories, tables of contents, and glossaries.

- *Intradocument* linking works best on your own Web site, where you can create and control the markup.

  When you link to spots on someone else's Web site, you're at its manager's mercy. That person controls linkable spots. Your links will break if the site designer removes or renames any spot to which you link.

Naming link locations

To identify and create a location within a page for direct access from other links, use an empty anchor element with the name attribute, like this:

```
<a name="top"></a>
```

The anchor element that marks the spot doesn't affect the appearance of any surrounding content. You can mark spots wherever you need them without worrying about how your pages look (or change) as a result.

Linking to named locations

As we mention earlier, you can mark locations for direct access by links

- Within the same page
- Within the same Web site
- On other Web sites

Within the same page

Links can help users navigate a single Web page. Intradocument hyperlinks include such familiar features as

- Back to Top links
- Tables of contents

Chapter 7

Finding and Using Images

*W*eb-page designers use images to deliver important information, direct site navigation, and contribute to the overall look and feel of a Web page. But you have to use images properly or you risk reducing their effectiveness.

When used well, images are a key element of page design. When used poorly, they can make a page unreadable or inaccessible.

This chapter is a crash course in using images on Web pages. You find out which image formats are Web-friendly and how to use (X)HTML elements to add images to your Web pages. You also discover how to attach links to your images and how to create image maps for your Web page.

The Role of Images in a Web Page

Images in Web sites may be logos, clickable navigation aids, or display content; they may also make a page look prettier, or serve to unify or illustrate a page's theme. A perfect example of the many different ways images can enhance and contribute to Web pages is the White House home page at www. whitehouse.gov, shown in Figure 7-1, where you see the Presidential seal and photos used to good effect.

Figure 7-1:
The White
House Web
page uses
images in
a variety of
ways.

Creating Web-Friendly Images

You can create and save graphics in many ways, but only a few formats are actually appropriate for images that you intend to use on the Web. As you create Web-friendly images, you must account for file formats and sizes.

Often, graphics file formats are specific to operating systems or software applications. But you can't predict a visitor's computer and software (other than a Web browser). So you need images that anyone can view with any browser. This means you need to use *cross-platform* file formats that users can view with any version of Microsoft Windows, the Mac OS, or Linux.

Optimizing images

As you build graphics for your Web page, maintain a healthy balance between file quality and size. Webmonkey has two good tutorials on trimming image file sizes and optimizing entire sites for fast download. For tips and tricks that can help you build pages that download quickly, review these handy resources:

⊬ Optimizing Images

```
http://www.yourhtmlsource.com/
          optimisation/image
          optimisation.html
```

⊬ Optimizing Web Graphics

```
http://www.websiteoptimization.com/
          speed/12
```

Only these three compressed formats are suitable for general use on the Web:

- **Graphics Interchange Format (GIF):** Images saved as GIFs often are smaller than those saved in other file formats. GIF supports up to 256 colors only, so if you try to save an image created with millions of colors as a GIF, you lose image quality. GIF is the best format for less-complex, nonphotographic images, such as line art and clip art.

- **Joint Photographic Experts Group (JPEG):** The JPEG file format supports 24-bit color (millions of colors) and complex images, such as photographs. JPEG is cross-platform and application-independent. A good image-editing tool can help you tweak the compression so you can strike an optimum balance between image quality and image-file size.

- **Portable Network Graphics (PNG):** PNG is the latest cross-platform and application-independent image file format. It was developed to bring together the best of GIF and JPEG. PNG has the same compression as GIF but supports 24-bit color (and even 32-bit color) like that of JPEG.

Any good graphics-editing tool, such as those mentioned in Chapter 22, lets you save images in any of these formats. Experiment with them to see how converting a graphic from one format to another changes its appearance and file size, then choose whichever format produces the best results.

Table 7-1 shows guidelines for choosing a file format for images by type.

Table 7-1	Choosing the Right File Format	
File Format	*Best Used For*	*Watch Out*
GIF	Line art and other images with few colors and less detail.	Don't use this format if you have a complex image or photo.
JPEG	Photos and other images with millions of colors and lots of detail.	Don't use with line art. This format compromises too much quality when you compress the file.
PNG	Photos and other images with millions of colors and lots of detail.	Don't use with line art. PNG offers the best balance between quality and file size.

For a complete overview of graphics formats, visit

- Builder.com's "Examine Graphic Channels and Space"

    `http://builder.cnet.com/webbuilding/0-3883-8-4892140-1.html`

- Webmonkey's "Web Graphics Overview"

    `http://www.webmonkey.com/01/28/index1a.html`

Adding an Image to a Web Page

When an image is ready for the Web, you need to use the correct markup to add it to your page. But you need to know where to store your image as well.

Image location

You can store images for your Web site in several places. Image storage works best if it uses *relative* URLs (stored somewhere on the Web site with your other (X)HTML files). You can store images in the same root file as your (X)HTML files, which gets confusing if you have a lot of files, or you can create a `graphics` or `images` directory in the root file of your Web site.

Relative links connect resources from the same Web site. You use absolute links between resources on two different Web sites. Turn to Chapter 6 for a complete discussion of the differences between relative and absolute links.

Three compelling reasons to store images on your own site are

- ✔ **Control:** When the images are stored on your site, you have complete control over them. You know that your images aren't going to disappear or change, and you can work to optimize them.

- ✔ **Speed:** If you link to images on someone else's site, you never know when that site may go down or be unbelievably slow. Linking to images on someone else's site also causes the other site owner to pay for the bandwidth required to display it on your site.

- ✔ **Copyright:** If you link to images on another Web site to display them on your site, you may violate copyright law. (In this case, obtain permission from the copyright holder to store and display the images on your site.)

Using the <img /> element

The image (`<img />`) element is an *empty element* (sometimes called a *singleton tag*) that you place on the page where you want your image to go.

An empty element has only one tag, with neither a distinct opening nor closing tag.

The following markup places an image named `07fg02-cd.jpg`, which is saved in the same directory as the (X)HTML file, between two paragraphs:

```
<!DOCTYPE html PUBLIC "-//W3C//DTD XHTML 1.0 Transitional//EN"
                      "http://www.w3.org/TR/xhtml1/DTD/xhtml1-transitional.dtd">
<html xmlns="http://www.w3.org/1999/xhtml">
<head>
  <meta http-equiv="Content-Type" content="text/html; charset=ISO-8859-1" />
   <title>CDs at Work</title>
</head>
  <body>
  <h1>CD as a Storage Medium</h1>
  <p>CD-ROMs have become a standard storage option in today's computing world
     because they are inexpensive and easy to use.</p>
  <img src="07fg02-cd.jpg" />
   <p>To read from a CD, you only need a standard CD-ROM drive, but to create
      CDs, you need either a CD-R or a CD-R/W drive.</p>
   </body>
</html>
```

A Web browser replaces the `<img />` element with the image file provided as the value for the `src` attribute, as shown in Figure 7-2.

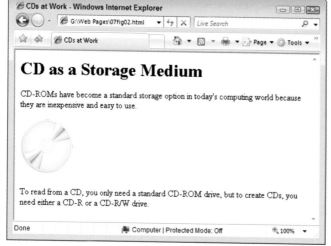

Figure 7-2:
Use the
<img />
element
to place
graphics in
a Web page.

The `src` attribute is like the `href` attribute that you use with an anchor (`<a>`) element. The `src` attribute specifies the location for the image you want to display on your page. The preceding example points to an image file in the same folder as the HTML file referencing it.

Adding alternative text

Alternative text describes an image so those who can't see the images for some reason can access that text to learn more about the image. Adding alternative text (often referred to by HTMLers as "alt text") is a good practice because it accounts for

- ✔ Visually impaired users who may not be able to see images and must rely on alternative text for a text-to-speech reader to read to them.

- ✔ Users who access the Web site from a phone browser with limited graphics capabilities.

- ✔ Users with slow modem connections who don't display images.

Some search engines and cataloguing tools use alternative text to index images.

Most of your users will see your images, but be prepared for those who won't. The (X)HTML specifications require that you provide alternative text to describe each image on a Web page. Use the `alt` attribute with the `<img />` element to add this information to your markup, like this:

```
<!DOCTYPE html PUBLIC "-//W3C//DTD XHTML 1.0 Transitional//EN"
                      "http://www.w3.org/TR/xhtml1/DTD/xhtml1-transitional.dtd">
<html xmlns="http://www.w3.org/1999/xhtml">
<head>
  <meta http-equiv="Content-Type" content="text/html; charset=ISO-8859-1" />
  <title>Inside the Orchestra</title>
</head>

<body>
  <p>Among the different sections of the orchestra you will find:</p>
  <p><img src="07fg03-violin.jpg" alt="violin " /> Strings</p>
  <p><img src="07fg03-trumpet.jpg" alt="trumpet" /> Brass</p>
  <p><img src="07fg03-woodwinds.jpg" alt="clarinet and saxophone" />
     Woodwinds</p>
</body>
</html>
```

When browsers don't display an image (or can't, as in text-only browsers such as Lynx), they display the alternative text instead, as shown in Figure 7-3. (We turned pictures off in IE to produce the screenshot.)

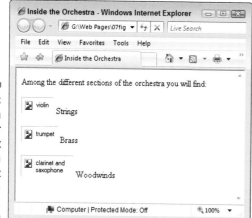

Figure 7-3:
When a
browser
doesn't
show an
image, it
shows alter-
native text.

When browsers show an image, some browsers — including Internet Explorer, Netscape, and Opera — show alternative text as pop-up tooltips when you hover your mouse pointer over an image for a few seconds, as shown in Figure 7-4. Firefox, however, does not.

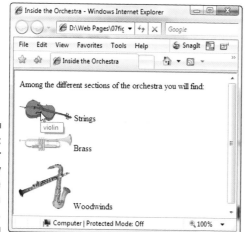

Figure 7-4:
A browser
may display
alternative
text as a
pop-up tip.

This means you can use alternative text either to describe the image to those who can't see it or to provide useful (or amusing) information about the image.

The W3C's Web Accessibility Initiative (WAI) includes helpful tips for creating useful and usable alternatives to visual content at

www.w3.org/TR/WCAG10-TECHS/#gl-provide-equivalents

Specifying image size

You can use the `height` and `width` attributes with the `<img />` element to let the browser know just how tall and wide an image is (in pixels):

```
<p><img src="07fg03-trumpet.jpg" width="50" height="70" alt="trumpet"
        />Brass</p>
```

Most browsers download the HTML and text associated with a page before they download the page graphics. Instead of making users wait for the whole page to download, browsers typically display the text first and then fill in graphics as they become available. If you tell the browser how big a graphic is, the browser can reserve a spot for it in the page display. This smooths the process of adding graphics to the Web page.

You can check the width and height of an image in pixels in any image-editing program, or in the image viewers built into Windows and the Mac OS. (You might be able simply to view the properties of the image in either Windows or the Mac OS to see its height and width.)

Another good use of the `height` and `width` attributes is to create colored lines on a page by using just a small colored square. For example, this markup adds a 10x10-pixel blue box to a Web page:

```
<img src="07fg05-blue-box.gif" alt="blue box" height="10" width="10" />
```

Use the `<img />` element `height` and `width` attributes to set image height and width. Thus we use these values to create 10x10 pixel blue box in a browser window (shown in Figure 7-5), even though the original image is 100x100 pixels in size. In general it's safe to reduce image dimensions using these attributes, though you'll always want to check the results carefully during testing (and with any kind of aspect sensitive image, you'll want to maintain its aspect ratio by dividing the original dimensions by some common value, as we did in going from 100x100 to 10x10, by dividing by 10).

Figure 7-5: A small box.

However, a change to the values for `height` and `width` in the markup turns this small blue box into a line 20 pixels high and 200 pixels wide:

```
<img src="07fg05-blue-box.gif" alt="blue box" height="20" width="200" />
```

The browser expands the image to fit the height and width specifics in the markup, as shown in Figure 7-6.

Figure 7-6:
A small box
becomes a
short line.

Using this technique, you can turn a single image like the blue box (only 1K in size) into a variety of lines — and even boxes:

- ✔ This can ensure that all dividers and other border elements on your page use the same color — they're all based on the same graphic.

- ✔ If you decide you want to change all your blue lines to green, you just change the image. Every line you've created changes colors.

When you specify a height and width for an image that are different from the image's actual height and width, you rely on the browser to scale the image display. This works great for single-color images such as the blue box, but it doesn't work well for images with multiple colors or images that display actual pictures. The browser doesn't size images well, and you wind up with a distorted picture. Figure 7-7 shows how badly a browser handles enlarging a trumpet image when the markup doubles the image height and width (note the jaggies on the trumpet bell, for example):

```
<p><img src="07fg03-trumpet.jpg" width="200" height="64" alt="trumpet" />
        Brass</p>
```

If you need several sizes for the same image — as for a logo or navigation button — use a large image as the master for that graphic, and make smaller versions; doing so gives you better control over the final look and feel of each image.

Figure 7-7:
Don't use a
browser to
resize
complex
images.

Setting an image border

By default, every image has a border of 1 — which doesn't show up in most browsers until you turn that image into a link (as shown in the "Images That Link" section later). You can use the `border` attribute with the `<img />` element to better control the border the browser displays around your image. This markup sets the border for the clarinet image to 10 pixels:

```
<img src="07fg03-woodwinds.jpg" width="100" height="83" alt="clarinet and
            saxophone" border="10" />
```

The browser uses this border on all four sides of the image, as in Figure 7-8.

Figure 7-8:
Use the bor-
der attribute
to create
a border
around your
image.

In Figure 7-8, the border is black and applies to all four sides of the image. If you want to control the color of the border or make the border appear differently on each side of the image, you have two options:

- Build the border into the image in an image-editing tool.
- Use Cascading Style Sheets (CSS), which we cover in Chapters 8 and 9.

Chapter 8

Introducing Cascading Style Sheets

The goal of *Cascading Style Sheets* (CSS) is to separate a Web page's style from its structure and to make it easier to maintain Web pages you've created. The structural elements of a page, such as headings (`<h1>` through `<h6>`) and body text, don't affect the look of those elements. By applying styles to those elements, you can *specify the element's layout on the page* and *add design attributes* (such as fonts, colors, and text indentation).

Style sheets give you precise control over how structural elements appear on a Web page. What's even better is that you can create one style sheet for an entire Web site to keep the layout and look of your content consistent from page to page. And here's the icing on this cake: Style sheets are easy to build and even easier to integrate into Web pages. In fact, you can add style markup to individual (X)HTML elements (called *inline style*), create sequences of style instructions in the head of an (X)HTML document (called an *internal style sheet*), or refer to a separate stand-alone style sheet using some kind of link or other reference (called an *external style sheet*) inside your (X)HTML document. In short, there are lots of ways to add style to a Web page!

As more Web sites transition to XHTML, the goal of the markup powers-that-be is to eventually *deprecate* (make obsolete) all formatting markup, such as the `<font>` element, from HTML's collection of elements. Someday, all presentation will belong to CSS.

When you want tight control over the display of your Web pages, style sheets are the way to go:

- ✔ Generally, style sheets give you more flexibility than markup can.
- ✔ Future HTML and XHTML elements will no longer include display-oriented tags.

Most modern browsers handle CSS well. However, some older browsers — such as Internet Explorer 4.0 and Netscape Navigator — have trouble displaying CSS correctly. Earlier browsers can't display CSS at all. If you know that many of your site's users still use one or more of these obsolete browsers, test your pages in these browsers; make sure they can read your pages.

Advantages of Style Sheets

HTML's formatting capabilities are limited, to say the least. When you design a page layout in HTML, you're limited to tables, font controls, and a few inline styles, such as bold and italic. *Style sheets* supply lots of tools to format Web pages with precise controls. With style sheets you can

- ✔ **Carefully control every aspect of page display:** Specify the amount of space between lines, character spacing, page margins, image placement, and more. You can also specify positioning of elements on your pages.

- ✔ **Apply changes globally:** You can guarantee consistent design across an entire Web site by applying the same style sheet to every Web page.

You can modify the look and feel of an entire site by changing just one document (the style sheet) instead of the markup on every page. Need to change the look of a heading? Redefine that heading's style attributes in the style sheet and save the sheet. The heading's look changes throughout your site. You can imagine one page after rapidly adopting the new look in a "cascade" of changes (hence the name) but that's just a metaphor; the cascade is instantaneous.

- ✔ **Instruct browsers to control appearance:** Provide Web browsers with more information about how you want your pages to appear than you can communicate using HTML.

- ✔ **Create dynamic pages:** Use JavaScript or another scripting language along with style sheets to create text and other content that moves, appears, or hides in response to user actions.

What CSS can do for a Web page

The gist of how style sheets work is as follows:

1. You define rules in a style sheet that specify how you want content described by a set of markup to appear.

   For example, you could specify that every first-level heading (`<h1>`) be displayed in purple Garamond 24-point type with a yellow background (not that you *would,* but you could).

2. You link style rules and markup.

3. The browser does the rest.

The current specification, CSS2.1, can

- ✐ Specify font type, size, color, and effects
- ✐ Set background colors and images
- ✐ Control many aspects of text layout, including alignment and spacing
- ✐ Set margins and borders
- ✐ Control list display
- ✐ Define table layout and display
- ✐ Automatically generate content for such standard page elements as counters and footers
- ✐ Control cursor display
- ✐ Define aural style sheets for text-to-speech browsers

CSS3: Next-generation style sheets

The next generation of CSS — CSS3 — is a collection of *modules* that address different aspects of Web-page formatting, such as fonts, background colors, lists, and text colors. The first of these modules became standards (officially called *Candidate Recommendations*) in mid-2004. But the majority of CSS3 modules aren't expected to become Candidate Recommendations until mid-2008 or later, and few browsers implement CSS3 features. In short, you don't need to worry about CSS3 — yet.

The W3C has devoted an entire section of its Web site to this topic at `www.w3.org/style/css`. You can find general CSS information there, as well as keep up with the status of CSS3. The site links to good CSS references and tutorials, and includes information on software packages that can make your style-sheet endeavors easier.

Property measurement values

Many HTML properties use measurement values. We tell you which measurement values go with which properties throughout this book. Standard property measurements dictate the size of a property in two ways.

Absolute value measurements can dictate a specific length or height with one of these values:

- ✓ **inches,** such as .5in

- ✓ **centimeters,** such as 3cm

- ✓ **millimeters,** such as 4mm

- ✓ **picas,** such as 1pc

    There are about six picas in an inch.

- ✓ **points,** such as 16pt

    There are 12 points in a pica.

- ✓ **pixels,** such as 13px (these match up to individual dots on your computer display).

Relative value measurements base length or height on a *parent element* value in the document:

- ✓ **p%:** A percentage of the current font-size value, such as 150%.

    For example, you can define a font size of 80% for all paragraphs. If your document body is defined with a 15-point font, the font size of the paragraphs is 12 points (80 percent of 15).

- ✓ **ex:** A value that is relative to the x-height of the current font. An x-height is the equivalent of the height of the lowercase character of a font, such as 1.5ex.

- ✓ **em:** A value that is relative to the current font size, such as 2em.

    Both 1em and 100% equal the current size.

Be careful when using these values; some properties support only some measurement values — length values, say, but not relative values. Don't let this jargon scare you. Just define the size in a value you're familiar with.

What you can do with CSS

You have a healthy collection of properties to work with as you write your style rules. You can control just about every aspect of a page's display — from borders to font sizes and everything in-between:

- ✓ **Background properties** control the background colors associated with blocks of text and with images. You can also use these properties to attach background colors to your page or to individual elements.

- ✓ **Border properties** control borders associated with the page, lists, tables, images, and block elements (such as paragraphs). You can specify border width, color, style, and distance from the element's content.

Using Different Kinds of Style Sheets

When you finish creating your style rules, you're ready to connect them to your HTML page with one of these options:

- **Insert style information into your document.** You can either

  - Use the `<style>` element to build a style sheet into a Web page.

    This is an *internal style sheet*.

  - Use the `style` attribute to add style information directly to a tag.

    This is an *inline style*.

- Use an *external style sheet*. You can either

  - Use the `<link>` tag to *link* your Web page to an external style sheet.

  - Use the CSS `@import` statement to *import* an external style sheet into the Web page.

Internal style sheets

An internal style sheet lives within your HTML page. Just add style rules to the `<style>` element in the document header. You can include as many (or as few) style rules as you want in an internal style sheet. (See Listing 8-1.)

Listing 8-1:   Adding an Internal Style Sheet to an HTML Document

```
<!DOCTYPE html PUBLIC "-//W3C//DTD XHTML 1.0 Transitional//EN"
        "http://www.w3.org/TR/xhtml1/DTD/xhtml1-transitional.dtd">
<html xmlns="http://www.w3.org/1999/xhtml">
<head>
  <title>Internal Style Sheet Example</title>
  <style type="text/css">
    body {background: black;
          color: white;
          font-size: 16px;
          font-family: Garamond;
          margin-left: 72px;
          margin-right: 72px;
          margin-top: 72px;}

    h1, h2, h3 {color: teal;
                font-family: Arial;
                font-size: 36px;}

    p.copyright {font-family: Arial;
```

(continued)

Listing 8-1 *(continued)*

```
                font-size: 12px;
                font-color: white;
                background: black;}

    .warning {font-family: Arial;
              font-size: 16px;
              font-color: red;}
  </style>
</head>
<body>

<!-- Document content goes here -->

</body>
</html>
```

The benefit of an internal style sheet is convenience: Your style rules are on the same page as your markup so you can tweak both quickly. But if you want the same style rules to control the appearance of more than one HTML page, move those styles from individual Web pages to an external style sheet.

External style sheets

An external style sheet holds all your style rules in a separate text document you can reference from any HTML file on your site. You must maintain a separate style sheet file, but an external style sheet offers benefits for overall site maintenance. If your site's pages use the same style sheet, you can change any formatting characteristic on all pages with a change to the style sheet.

We recommend using external style sheets on your sites.

Linking

To reference an external style sheet, use the `link` element in the Web page header, like this:

```
<html>
<head>
  <title>External Style Sheet Example</title>
  <link rel="stylesheet" type="text/css" href="styles.css" />
<head>
<body>

<!-- Document content goes here -->

</body>
</html>
```

Figure 9-1:
This style-
free page
doesn't
maximize
this cat's
possibilities.

Visual layouts

Instead of the links appearing above the image, as they are in Figure 9-1, we
want them on the left, a typical location for navigation tools. The following
markup floats the text for the search site links to the left of the image:

```
<style type="text/css">
  .navbar {
    background-color: #CCC;
    border-bottom: #999;
    border-left: #999;
    border-width: 0 0 thin thin;
    border-style: none none groove groove;
    display: block;
    float: left;
    margin: 0 0 0 10px;
    padding: 0 10px 0 10px;
    width: 100px;
  }
</style>
```

In the preceding rules, we

- ✔ Added a `<style>` element
- ✔ Defined the `navbar` class inside the `<style>` element
- ✔ Used the `navbar` class to instruct the content to float to the left of images, which causes them to appear in the same part of the page to the left, rather than above the graphic.

This rule says that anything on the page that belongs to the `navbar` class (as shown in Figure 9-2) should display with

- ✔ A light-gray background
- ✔ A thin grooved-line border at bottom and left, in a darker gray
- ✔ No top or right border
- ✔ A block that floats to the left (so everything else on the page moves right, as with the image in Figure 9-2)
- ✔ A left margin of 10 pixels
- ✔ Padding at top and bottom of 10 pixels each
- ✔ A navbar area 100 total pixels wide

Figure 9-2: The navigation bar now looks more like standard left-hand navigation.

Note that several properties in the declaration, called shorthand properties, take multiple values, such as `margin` and `padding`. Shorthand properties collect values from multiple related CSS properties (such as `margin-height`, `margin-width`, and so forth). See our online materials for a complete list.

Those values correspond to settings for the top, right, bottom, and left edges of the navbar's box. margin creates an empty zone around the box, and pad-ding defines the space between the edges or borders of the box and the content inside the box. Here are the rules that explain how to associate values with properties that deal with margins, borders, padding, and so forth:

- ✔ If all the sides have the same value, a single value works.

- ✔ If *any* side is different from the others, *every* side needs a separate value. It's okay to set some or all of these values to zero as you see fit; this can often help to ensure that pages display consistently across a wider range of browsers (and browser versions).

To remember what's what, think of the edges of an element box in clockwise order, starting with the top edge: top, right, bottom, and then left.

Positioning

CSS provides several ways to specify exactly where an element should appear on a page. These controls use various kinds of positioning based on the relationships between an element's box and its parent element's box to help page designers put page elements where they want them to go. The kinds of properties involved are discussed in the following sections.

Location

You can control the horizontal and vertical location of an image. But when you use absolute positioning with any page element, you instruct that element exactly where it must sit, relative to the upper left corner of the browser window. Thus, instead of letting it be drawn automatically to the right of the navigation bar, you can place an image down and to the left, as in Figure 9-3:

```
#theCat {position: absolute; top: 100px; left: 100px;}
```

You might be wondering why the navbar rule starts with a period, and the theCat rule starts with a pound symbol (also known as a hash mark or octothorpe). That's because the period applies to a class attribute, but the pound symbol applies to an id attribute. You can apply either a class or an id to specific elements; the difference between these two is that a class can be used repeatedly, but an id can appear only once on a page. You can't have anything else on the page that uses theCat as its id. The difference, quite simply, is that a class lets you refer to some entire kind of element with a single reference, but an id can address only a single instance of an element.

Overlapping

Two objects *can* be assigned to the same position in a Web page. When that happens, the browser must decide the display order and which objects to show and which ones to hide.

Figure 9-3:
The image
is more
striking
in this
location.

The `z-index`, added to any rule, tells CSS how you want any object stacked over and under other objects that occupy the same space on the page:

- Lower numbers move down the stack.
- Higher numbers move up the stack.
- The default value for `z-index` is `auto`, which means it's the same as for its parent element.

Giving `theCat` a `z-index` value of `-1` automatically puts it behind everything else on the page (as shown in Figure 9-4) for which the `z-index` isn't set.

Fonts

You can make a page more interesting by replacing old boring default fonts. Start by specifying a generic body font as well as setting some other default rules, such as background color and text color.

Body text

Here's an example that sets the style for text within the `body` tag:

```
body {font-family: verdana, geneva, arial, helvetica, sans-serif;
      font-size: 12px; line-height: 16px; background-color: white;
      color: teal;}
```

Figure 9-4:
The cat's
peeking out
from behind
the naviga-
tion bar.

Because the `body` element holds all content for any Web page, this affects everything on the page. The preceding rule instructs the browser to show all text that appears within the `body` element as follows:

- ✔ The text is rendered using one of the fonts listed. We placed Verdana at the head of the list because it is the preferred choice, and browsers check for available fonts in the order listed. (Note that a generic font, in this case `sans-serif`, almost always appears last in such lists because the browser can almost always supply such a font itself.)

  You can list more than one font. The browser uses the first font in your list that's available in the browser. For example, the browser looks for fonts from our list in this order:

  1. Verdana
  2. Geneva
  3. Arial
  4. Helvetica
  5. The browser's default sans-serif font

- ✔ 12-pixel font size
- ✔ 16-pixel line height

  The lines are spaced as though the fonts are 16 pixels high, so there's more vertical space between lines.

Figure 9-5 shows that

- ✔ All changes apply to the entire page, including the navigation bar.

- ✔ The `font-family` changes in the `h1` heading, but neither the `font-size` nor `line-height` changes for that heading.

  Because headers have specific defaults for `font-size` and `line-height`, another rule is needed to modify them.

In shooting Figure 9-5, the HTML used for our screen capture includes an additional tweak for IE. That's because a bug in Internet Explorer for Windows that doesn't occur in other browsers causes heading (`h1`) text to get truncated at the top. (Try the source (X)HTML for Figure 9-5 in IE to see what we mean; we had to add CSS markup that set `line-height: 105%;` for h1 to create this display.) Unfortunately, CSS rendering can be unpredictable enough that you must test style rules in various browsers to see how they look — and then tweak accordingly.

Figure 9-5:
The fonts
are nicer,
but they
could still
use a little
more work.

Headings

If we explicitly assign style properties to the `h1` element, display results are more predictable. Here's a sample set of styles:

```
h1 {font-family: "trebuchet ms", verdana, geneva, arial, helvetica, sans-serif;
    font-size: 24px; line-height: 26px;}
```

Figure 9-6 shows a first-level heading using the font family and type size that we want: 24-pixel Trebuchet MS, with a 26-pixel line height. If we didn't have the Trebuchet MS font on our system, the heading would appear in Verdana.

When a font name includes spaces (like `trebuchet ms` or `times new roman`), the full name must be within quotation marks. (See Chapter 8 for more information.)

Figure 9-6:
Declaring
a rule for
h1 makes
it appear
just how we
like it.

Hyperlinks

We think that having the hyperlinks underlined — which is normal — makes the menu look a little cluttered. Luckily, we can turn underlines off with CSS, but we still want the hyperlinks to look like hyperlinks, so we tell CSS to

- Make links bold.
- Make underlines appear when the cursor is over a link.
- Show links in certain colors.

The following style rules define how a browser should display hyperlinks:

```
a {text-decoration: none; font-weight: bold}
a:link {color: blue}
a:visited {color: #93C}
a:hover {text-decoration: underline}
```

What's going on here? Starting from the top, we're setting two rules for the `<a>` tag that apply to all links on the page:

- ✔ **The** `text-decoration` **declaration sets its value to** `none`.

  This gets rid of the underlining for all the links.

- ✔ **The** `font-weight` **declaration has a value of** `bold`.

  This makes all the links on the page appear in bold.

The remaining rules in the preceding code are *pseudo class selectors*. Their most common usage is to modify how links appear in their different states. (For more information on pseudo classes, see Chapter 10.) Here we change the color when a link has been visited, and we turn underlining on when the mouse pointer hovers over link text — doing so identifies hyperlinks when the cursor is in clicking range. Figure 9-7 shows how the page appears when the previous style rules are applied.

Figure 9-7:
The final
version of
our page.

Externalizing style sheets

When the final page is the way you want it, you're ready to cut and paste your tested, approved, internal style sheet into an external style sheet.

- ✔ Every page of the site can use the whole style sheet with the addition of only one line of code to each page.

- ✔ Changes can be made site-wide with one change in the external style sheet.

To create an external style sheet from a well-tested, internal style sheet, follow these steps:

1. **Copy all text that sits between the** `<style>` **and** `</style>` **tags.**

2. **Paste that text into its own new document.**

   This text should include only CSS markup, without any HTML tags or markup.

3. **Add a** `.css` **suffix to the document's name (for example,** `myStyles.css`**) when saving.**

   The suffix shows at a glance that it's a CSS file.

So you've got your external style sheet. Time now to link your HTML file to said external style sheet. You have two options available to you:

✔ **Use the** `<link>` **tag.**

   All CSS-capable browsers understand the `link` tag.

✔ **Use the** `<style>` **tag with the** `@import` **keyword.**

   Only newer browsers understand the `<style>` and `@import` combination.

See Chapter 8 for more on these two methods.

Style sheets for old and new browsers

To include rules that both old and new browsers can handle, you can create *two* style sheets for a site:

✔ A basic style sheet that contains only the simplest of styles

✔ A complex style sheet that uses the capabilities of the most powerful new browsers

The following code uses two style sheets:

```
<link href="simpleStyles.css" rel="stylesheet" type="text/css" />
<style type="text/css">
  @import "complexStyles.css";
</style>
```

Here's how that works:

✔ A `<link>` tag brings in `simpleStyles.css`, a basic style sheet for old browsers.

✔ The `<style>` tag and `@import` keyword combination brings in `complexStyles.css`, a complex style sheet for new browsers, which overrides the styles in `simpleStyles.css`.

Both old and new browsers get exactly the rules they can handle.

Multimedia

You can specify how you want your Web pages to look or behave on different *media types* depending on the medium.

Table 9-1 lists all the media types and their uses.

Table 9-1	Recognized Media Types
Media Type	*Description*
all	Suitable for all devices
aural	For speech synthesizers
braille	For Braille tactile-feedback devices
embossed	For paged Braille printers
handheld	For handheld devices (such as those with a small screen, monochrome monitor, and limited bandwidth)
print	For paged, opaque material and for documents viewed on-screen but in Print Preview mode
projection	For projected presentations such as projectors or transparencies
screen	For color computer screens
tty	For media that use a fixed-pitch character grid such as teletypes, terminals, or portable devices with limited display capabilities
tv	For television-type devices (such as those with low resolution, color capability, limited-scrollability screens, and some sound available)

CSS can make changes to customize how the same pages

🖝 Render on a computer screen

🖝 Print on paper

A nifty color background might make your page a mess when it's printed on a black-and-white laser printer, but proper use of print-media styles can keep this sort of thing from happening!

🖝 Sound when read out loud

Visual media styles

Table 9-2 lists the CSS properties that you're most likely to use in a typical Web page. Our online content for this book includes brief descriptions of the most commonly used CSS properties and (X)HTML tags and attributes.

Table 9-2	**Visual Media Styles**		
Property	*Values*	*Default Value*	*Description*
back-ground-color	Any color, by name or hex code	transparent	Background color of the page
back-ground-image	URL	none	URL of an image to display in a page background
color	Any color, by name or hex code	Up to you!	Color of the foreground text
font-family	Any named font cursive fantasy monospace sans-serif serif	Up to you!	Font to display
font-size	Number + unit xx-small x-small small medium large x-large xx-large	medium	Size of the font to be displayed
font-weight	normal bold bolder lighter	normal	Weight (how bold or light) the font should appear
line-height	normal number + unit	normal	Vertical spacing between lines of text
text-align	left right center justify	Up to you + normal text direction	Which way the text on the page should be aligned

continued

Table 9-2 *(continued)*

Property	Values	Default Value	Description
list-style-image	URL	none	URL of an image to display as the bullets for a list
list-style-position	inside outside	outside	Wrapping the list text inside or outside of bullet points
list-style-type	disc circle square decimal decimal-leading-zero lower-alpha upper-alpha none	disc	Bullet type on lists
display	block inline none	inline	Format of a defined section of the page
top	Percentage number + unit auto	auto	For absolutely positioned objects, the offset from the top edge of the positioning context
right	Percentage number + unit auto	auto	For absolutely positioned objects, the offset from the right edge of the positioning context
bottom	Percentage number + unit auto	auto	For absolutely positioned objects, the offset from the bottom edge of the positioning context
left	Percentage number + unit auto	auto	For absolutely positioned objects, the offset from the left edge of the positioning context

Property	Values	Default Value	Description
position	static absolute relative fixed	static	Method by which an element box is laid out, relative to positioning context
visibility	collapse visible hidden inherit	inherit	Indicates whether an object will be displayed on the page
z-index	Number auto	auto	Stacking order of an object
border-style	none dotted dashed solid double groove ridge inset outset	Not defined	The displayed style of an object's borders Can be broken out into border-top-style, border-right-style, border-bottom-style, and border-left-style
border-width	thin medium thick Number	Not defined	Width of the border around an object Can be broken out into border-top-width, border-right-width, border-bottom-width, and border-left-width
border-color	Any color, by name or hex code transparent	Not defined	Color of an object's border Can be broken out into border-top-color, border-right-color, border-bottom-color, and border-left-color

continued

Table 9-2 (continued)

Property	Values	Default Value	Description
float	left right none	none	Specifies whether the object should be floated to one side of the document
height	Percentage number + unit auto	auto	Displayed height of an object
width	Percentage number + unit auto	auto	Displayed width of an object
margin	Percentage number + unit auto	Not defined	Displayed margins of an object Can be broken out into margin-top, margin-right, margin-bottom, and margin-left
padding	Percentage number + unit auto	Not defined	Displayed blank space around an object Can be broken out into padding-top, padding-right, padding-bottom, and padding-left
cursor	auto crosshair default pointer move text help	auto	Cursor appearance in the browser window

Some browsers don't support all CSS properties. If you're using CSS features, test your pages with the browsers that you expect your visitors will use.

If you want to take an extremely thorough guide to CSS everywhere you go, put it on your iPod! Westciv's free podGuide is a folder of small text files. Download the zipped file and follow the instructions on how to install it, and you have complete documentation with you at all times. (You also win the title of "World's Biggest CSS Geek.") The podGuide is at

```
www.westciv.com/news/podguide.html
```

Paged media styles

CSS can customize how a page looks when it's printed. We recommend these guidelines:

✏ Replace sans-serif fonts with serif fonts.

  Serif fonts are easier to read in print than sans-serif fonts.

✏ Insert advertisements that

  • Make sense when they aren't animated

  • Are useful without clicking

Aural (speech-sound) styles

Aural browsers and styles aren't just for the visually impaired. They're also useful for Web users who

✏ Have reading problems

✏ Need information while driving

The following example recommends voices to be played using male and female characters to make it clear which characters are speaking:

```
<style>
    @media aural {
        p.stanley {voice-family: male;}
        p.stella {voice-family: female;}
    }
</style>
```

Usually you don't have to worry much about adding aural styles to your page. The default readers should work just fine if

✏ Your page is mostly text.

✏ You don't have a strong opinion about how it sounds, so that any clearly male or female voice will do.

That said, you can find a complete listing of all aural style properties on this book's companion Web site.

In general, paged media styles help ensure that text looks as good when it's printed as it does in a Web browser. Paged media styles also help you hide irrelevant content when pages are printed (banners, ads, and so forth), thus reducing wasted paper and user frustration. See Table 9-3 for an explanation of paged media properties in CSS that you can use to help your users make the most when printing Web pages.

Table 9-3		Paged Media Styles	
Property	*Values*	*Default Value*	*Description*
orphans	Number	2	The minimum number of lines in a paragraph that must be left at the bottom of a page
page-break-after	auto always avoid left right	auto	The page-breaking behavior after an element
page-break-before	auto always avoid left right	auto	The page-breaking behavior before an element
page-break-inside	auto avoid	auto	The page-breaking behavior inside an element
widows	Number	2	The minimum number of lines in a paragraph that must be left at the top of a page

The example in Listing 9-2 uses these options for paged media styles:

   ✔ Make the output black text on a white background.

   ✔ Replace sans-serif fonts with serif fonts.

Listing 9-2: Adding a Print Style Sheet

```
<!DOCTYPE html PUBLIC "-//W3C//DTD XHTML 1.0 Transitional//EN"
   "http://www.w3.org/TR/xhtml1/DTD/xhtml1-transitional.dtd">
<html xmlns="http://www.w3.org/1999/xhtml">
<head>
<title>This is my page</title>
<meta http-equiv="Content-Type" content="text/html; charset=ISO-8859-1" />
<style>
   body {background-color: black; color: white; font-family: sans-serif;}

   @media print {
     body {background-color: white; color: black; font-family: serif}
   }
</style>
</head>
<body>
   This page will look very different when sent to the printer.
</body>
</html>
```

If you're now wondering why none of the properties in Table 9-3 were set, but other properties were, it's because (in this example) their defaults worked fine. And just because those page properties can be set doesn't mean that you can't set other properties also — it isn't an either/or.

Chapter 10

Getting Creative with Colors and Fonts

In This Chapter

▷ Using CSS to define text formatting

▷ Working with page colors and backgrounds

▷ Changing font display

▷ Adding text treatments

*B*efore style sheets came along, you had to rely on HTML markup to control backgrounds, colors, fonts, and text sizes on Web pages. With style sheets on the scene, however, designers could now separate style information from content — meaning they could use Cascading Style Sheets (CSS) to control font, color, and other style information.

Why bother? Simple. When you use CSS, you get the following:

✐ Better control when updating or editing formatting information.

✐ No more HTML documents cluttered with `<font>` tags.

✐ More options for formatting text, such as defining line height, font weight, and text alignment, and converting text to *uppercase* (capital letters) or lowercase characters.

(X)HTML still includes a few formatting elements, such as `<tt>`, `<i>`, `<big>`, `<b>`, and `<small>`; however, the remaining formatting elements, such as `<font>`, are *deprecated*. That means they're no longer recommended for use (although they still work, and most browsers recognize them). We don't think you should use them anymore, but that decision is yours to make.

Color Values

(X)HTML defines color values in two ways:

- By *name* (you choose from a limited list)
- By *number* (harder to remember, but you have many more options)

Color names

The HTML specification includes 16 color names that you can use to define colors in your pages. Table 10-1 shows these colors below (the numbers that start with the hash mark # are in *hexadecimal* notation, a mix of the letters A–F (for 10 through 15) and the more typical 0–9 we all know and love from decimal numbers.

Table 10-1: Named color values in (X)HTML

Color name	#RGB code	color
Black	#000000	
Silver	#C0C0C0	
Gray	#808080	
White	#FFFFFF	
Maroon	#800000	
Red	#FF0000	
Purple	#800080	
Fuchsia	#FF00FF	
Green	#008000	
Lime	#00FF00	
Olive	#808000	
Yellow	#FFFF00	
Navy	#000080	
Blue	#0000FF	
Teal	#008080	
Aqua	#00FFFF	

Line height

The *line height* of a paragraph is the amount of space between each line within the paragraph.

Line height is like line spacing in a word processor.

To alter the amount of space between lines of a paragraph, use the line-height property:

```
selector {line-height: value;}
```

The value of the line-height property can be either

- ✔ One of the standard font property measurement values (listed in Chapter 8)
- ✔ A number that multiplies the element's font size, such as 1.5

We assign a quotation class to the first paragraph throughout this chapter so you can see the changes. This allows us to apply these styles to the first paragraph by using

```
<p class="quotation">
```

in the HTML document.

The following rules style the first paragraph in italics, indent that paragraph, and increase the line height to increase readability (see Figure 10-3):

```
body {color: #808000; font-family: Verdana, sans-serif; font-size: 85%;}
.quotation {font-style: italic; text-indent: 10pt; line-height: 150%;}
```

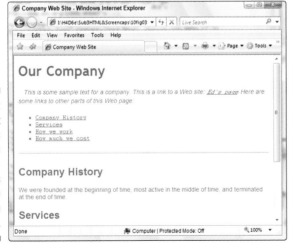

Figure 10-3: Any element that belongs to the quotation class gets the same formatting.

Character spacing

You can *increase* or *reduce* the amount of spacing between letters or words by using these properties:

- ✔ `word-spacing`: The style declaration for `word-spacing` is

  ```
  selector {word-spacing: value;}
  ```

  Designers call the space between words *tracking*.

- ✔ `letter-spacing`: The style declaration for `letter-spacing` is

  ```
  selector {letter-spacing: value;}
  ```

  Designers call the space between letters *kerning*.

The value of either spacing property must be a *length* defined by a standard font property measurement value (listed in Chapter 8).

The following code increases the letter spacing (kerning) of the first paragraph (see Figure 10-4):

```
body {color: #808000; font-family: Verdana, sans-serif; font-size: 85%;}
.quotation {font-style: italic; text-indent: 10pt; letter-spacing: 6px;}
```

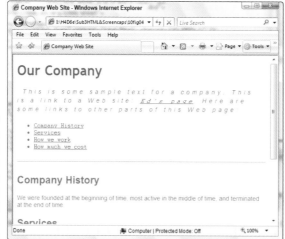

Figure 10-4: Kerning can be larger or smaller than the font's normal spacing.

Positioning

Alignment properties allow you to control how the edges of text blocks line up against one another (otherwise known as "edge alignment").

Alignment

Alignment determines whether the left and right sides of a text block are

- **Flush:** Starting or ending together
- **Ragged:** Starting or ending at different points

Syntax

Alignment is defined with the `text-align` property. The style declaration to align text is as follows:

```
selector {text-align: value;}
```

The value of the `text-align` property must be one of the following keywords:

- `left` **aligns the text to the left.** The right side of the text block is *ragged*.
- `right` **aligns the text to the right.** The left side of the text block is *ragged*.
- `center` **centers the text in the middle of the window.** Both sides of the text block are *ragged*.
- `justify` **aligns the text for both the left and right side.** The spacing within the text in each line is adjusted so both sides of the text block are *flush*.

Justifying text affects letter or word spacing in the paragraph. Test the results before displaying your Web pages to the world.

Markup

The following example defines the alignment for the first-level heading and the first paragraph (see Figure 10-5):

```
body {color: #808000; font-family: Verdana, sans-serif; font-size: 85%;}
h1 {color: teal; font-family: "Trebuchet MS", Arial, Helvetica, sans-serif;
    font-weight: 800; font-size: 24pt; line-height: 30 pt; text-align: center}
.quotation {font-style: italic; text-indent: 10pt; text-align: left;}
```

Indent

You can define the amount of space that should precede the first line of a paragraph by using the `text-indent` property.

This doesn't indent the whole paragraph. That requires CSS box properties, such as `margin-left` and `margin-right` (see Chapter 9).

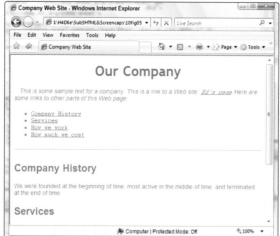

Figure 10-5:
The first-
level
heading is
centered;
the first
paragraph
is aligned to
the left.

Syntax

The style declaration used to indent text is

```
selector {text-indent: value;}
```

Here `value` must be one of the standard length-property measurement values (listed in Chapter 8).

Markup

As seen in this chapter, the `quotation` class has a `text-indent` of 10 points.

```
body {color: #808000; font-family: Verdana, sans-serif; font-size: 85%;}
.quotation {font-style: italic; text-indent: 10pt;}
```

Text treatments

CSS allows you to decorate your text by using boldface, italics, underline, overline, or line-through, and even allows your text to blink (when that's supported by browsers).

Bold

Using a boldface font is one of the more common text embellishments a designer uses. To apply boldface in HTML, use the <b> tag. However, CSS provides you with more control over the font weight of the bolded text.

Syntax

This style declaration uses the `font-weight` property:

```
selector {font-weight: value;}
```

The value of the `font-weight` property may be one of the following:

- ✔ `bold`: Renders the text in an average bold weight

- ✔ `bolder`: Relative value that renders a font weight bolder than the current weight (possibly assigned by a parent element)

- ✔ `lighter`: Relative value that renders a font weight lighter than the current weight (possibly assigned by a parent element)

- ✔ `normal`: Removes any bold formatting

- ✔ One of these integer values: `100` (lightest), `200`, `300`, `400` (normal), `500`, `600`, `700` (standard bold), `800`, `900` (darkest)

Markup

The following example bolds hyperlinks (see Figure 10-6), and turns the underline off and changes the color to green once a link is visited (we did this to the Company History item to show you what it looks like):

```
body {color: black; font-family: Arial, Verdana, sans-serif; font-size: 85%;}
a {font-weight: bold;}
a:link {color: olive; text-decoration: underline;}
a:visited {color: green; text-decoration: none;}
```

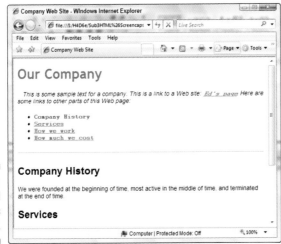

Figure 10-6:
All
hyperlinks
are bolded.

Italic

Italics are commonly used to set off quotations or to emphasize text. To apply italics in HTML, use the `<i>` tag. However, CSS provides you with more control over the font style of text through the `font-style` property.

Syntax

This style declaration uses the `font-style` property:

```
selector {font-style: value;}
```

The value of the `font-style` property may be one of the following:

- `italic`: Renders the text in *italics* (a special font that usually *slants*).
- `oblique`: Renders the text as *oblique* (a slanted version of the normal font).
- `normal`: Removes any italic or oblique formatting.

Markup

The following example assigns an italic font style to the first-level heading:

```
body {color: #808000; font-family: Verdana, sans-serif; font-size: 85%;}
h1 {color: teal; font-family: "MS Trebuchet", Arial, Helvetica, sans-serif;
          text-transform: uppercase;
     font-style: italic; font-weight: 800; font-size: 24pt; line-height: 30pt;
          text-align: center;}
```

Capitalization

You use the `text-transform` property to set capitalization in your document.

Syntax

This style declaration uses the `text-transform` property:

```
selector {text-transform: value;}
```

The value of the `text-transform` property may be one of the following:

- `capitalize`: Capitalizes the first character in every word.
- `uppercase`: Renders all letters of the text of the specified element in uppercase.
- `lowercase`: Renders all letters of the text of the specified element in lowercase.
- `none`: Keeps the value of the inherited element.

Markup

The following example renders the first-level heading in uppercase (shown in Figure 10-7):

```
body {color: #808000; font-family: Verdana, sans-serif; font-size: 85%;}
h1 {color: #808000; font-family: Arial, Helvetica, sans-serif;
    font-weight: 800; font-size: 24pt;
    text-align: center; text-transform: uppercase;}
```

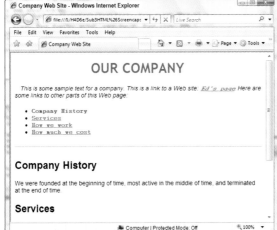

Figure 10-7:
The first-
level
heading is
rendered
in all
uppercase.

The text-decoration property

The `text-decoration` property allows for text formatting that's a tad crazier. It isn't used often.

Syntax

This style declaration uses the `text-decoration` property:

```
selector {text-decoration: value;}
```

The value of the `text-decoration` property may be one of the following:

- `underline`: Underlines text.

- `overline`: Renders the text with a line over it.

- `line-through`: Renders the text with a line through it.

- `blink`: Blinks the text on the screen.

    Are you *sure* you want blinking text?

    - `blink` isn't supported by all browsers.

    - `blink` can be dreadfully annoying and distracting.

- `none`: Removes any text decoration.

Markup

The following example changes the link when the mouse hovers over it. In this case, it turns off any underlining for a link:

```
body {color: #808000; font-family: Verdana, sans-serif; font-size: 85%;}
a:link {color: olive; text-decoration: underline;}
a:visited {color: olive; text-decoration: underline;}
a:hover {color: olive; text-decoration: none;}
```

The catchall font property

Many font properties can be summarized in one style declaration by using the shorthand `font` property. When it's used, only one style rule is needed to define a combination of font properties:

```
selector {font: value value value;}
```

The value of the `font` property is a list of any values that correspond to the various font properties:

- The following values must be defined in the following order, though they need not be consecutive:

  - `font-size` (required)

  - `line-height` (optional)

  - `font-family` (required)

- The `font-family` value list must end with a semicolon.

- Use commas to separate multiple font family names.

- The following values are optional and may occur in any order within the declaration. Individual values are separated by spaces:

  - `font-style`

  - `font-variant`

  - `font-weight`

For example, you can use the following style declaration to create a specific style for a first-level heading:

```
h1 {font: italic bold 150% Arial, Helvetica, sans-serif;}
```

When using tables for layout, without visible borders, it doesn't matter much which attribute you use. However, if you add color to your tables — or use a border for any reason — you can see a considerable difference. That's because cellpadding increases the space within the border, and cellspacing increases the width of the border itself, as shown clearly in Figures 11-7 and 11-8.

The default value for cellpadding is 1; the default for cellspacing is 2. If you don't define cellpadding and cellspacing, your users' browsers assume the defaults. Accounting for those pixels in your sketch is a good idea, unless you set those values explicitly to zero.

Figure 11-7:
The cell-padding attribute increases the space within each cell (here it's set to 20).

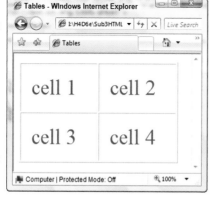

Figure 11-8:
The cell-spacing attribute increases the width of the border (here it's also set to 20).

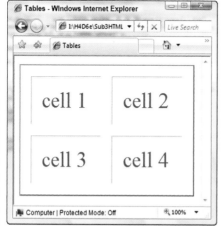

Working with `cellpadding` and `cellspacing` to get your table layout just right can be a bit of a headache. Sometimes you need to create empty cells to help control layout. Although this trick is a bit of a workaround, many designers use it. You just

1. **Create a cell.**
2. **Fill the cell with either one of these:**

   - `<br />`
   - A spacer image (a transparent `.gif` that is 1×1 pixel) with which you can manipulate the width

CSS

You can use CSS to control cell padding and spacing between cells.

Within cells

To control the padding within cells, you use the `padding` property, like so:

```
selector {padding: value;}
```

The value for the `padding` property must be defined by an absolute or relative length, or percentage.

To set the padding of a table cell, use the following style declaration:

```
td {padding: 10px;}
```

The `padding` property can be used with most (X)HTML elements. For example, if you created a footer and assigned it a class name, you can define padding for the element using the following style rule:

```
.footer { padding: 5px;}
```

Between cells

You can control the spacing between your cells using the `border-spacing` property:

```
selector {border-spacing: value;}
```

The value for the `border-spacing` property must be defined by an absolute or relative length, or percentage:

To set the padding of a table cell, use the following style declaration:

```
td {padding: 10px;}
```

The border-spacing property can be used only in conjunction with the <td> element.

Shifting alignment

If you use tables to define your layout, you need to control their placement in the browser window. You can do this by using (X)HTML or CSS.

You use attributes that are part of the HTML standard to align your tables (horizontally) and your table contents (horizontally and vertically).

Aligning tables is similar to aligning images.

Horizontal alignment

You can horizontally align cell contents using the align attribute in various table elements.

✔ To align your table horizontally, use the align attribute with the <table> element.

The align attribute, when used with the <table> element, has the following possible values: left, right, or center of the document.

✔ You can use the align attribute with the <td> (cell) or <tr> (row) elements to align text within the cell or row.

The values that can be used with the align attribute in the <td> or <tr> elements are

• align="right": Aligns the table or cell contents against the right side.

• align="left": Aligns the table or cell contents against the left side. (This is the default setting.)

• align="center": Centers the table or cell contents. When applied to the <table>element, it centers the table, when applied to table cells it centers their contents.

• align="justify": Justifies cell contents in the middle (not widely supported).

• align="char": Aligns cell contents around a specific character (not widely supported).

The following example aligns a table in the center of the page, with centered text in each cell (see Figure 11-9):

```
<!DOCTYPE html PUBLIC "-//W3C//DTD XHTML 1.0 Transitional//EN"
    "http://www.w3.org/TR/xhtml1/DTD/xhtml1-transitional.dtd">
<html xmlns="http://www.w3.org/1999/xhtml">
<head>
    <title>Tables</title>
</head>
<body>
 <table border="2" width="430" align="center" cellpadding="20">
  <tr>
    <td width="630" colspan="2" align="center"> contents </td>
  </tr>
  <tr>
    <td width="230" align="center"> contents </td>
    <td width="200" align="center"> contents </td>
  </tr>
 </table>
</body>
</html>
```

Vertical alignment

You can vertically align cell contents by using the `valign` attribute. It can only be used with the `<tr>` (cell) and `<td>` (row) elements.

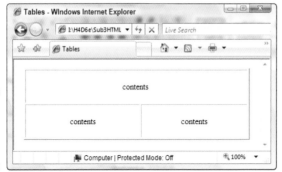

Figure 11-9:
A simple
table
centered.

The possible values are

- ✔ `valign="top"`: Vertically aligns cell contents to the top of the cell.
- ✔ `valign="bottom"`: Vertically aligns cell contents to the bottom of the cell.
- ✔ `valign="middle"`: Vertically centers the cell contents. (This is the default.)
- ✔ `valign="baseline"`: Defines a baseline for all other cells in the same row, so alignment is the same for all cells.

You can also use the `align` and `valign` attributes with the following table elements: `<col>`, `<colgroup>`, `<tbody>`, `<tfoot>`, `<th>`, and `<thead>`.

If you set alignment for a row (`<tr>`) and then set alignment for a cell within that row (`<td>`), the setting for the cell overrides the setting for the row.

You might as well get used to hearing that most X(HTML) formatting attributes are deprecated in favor of CSS. However, even though the `align` attribute is deprecated for most (X)HTML elements, it is still OK when used with table elements.

You can't use the `valign` attribute with the `<table>` tag.

Using CSS to define alignment

There are two CSS properties you can use to control table alignment using CSS: `text-align` and `vertical-align`. They function just like the preceding `align` and `valign` attributes.

To use the `text-align` property, assign it one of the following values:

- ✔ `right`: Aligns the table or cell contents against the right side.
- ✔ `left`: Aligns the table or cell contents against the left side. (This is the default.)
- ✔ `center`: Centers the table or cell contents.
- ✔ `justify`: Justifies cell contents in the middle.

To use the `vertical-align` property, assign it one of the following values:

- ✔ `top`: Vertically aligns cell contents to the top of the cell.
- ✔ `bottom`: Vertically aligns cell contents to the bottom of the cell.
- ✔ `middle`: Vertically centers the cell contents. (This is the default.)
- ✔ `baseline`: Defines a baseline for all other cells in the same row, so alignment is the same for all cells.

You can control the alignment of an entire row by assigning alignment properties to the `<tr>` element.

You can't center a table by using the `text-align` property — it's only for text alignment. Currently, you have a few options for centering the entire table. None of them is ideal, but they all work:

✔ Use the deprecated `<center>` tags around the table (not advised).

✔ Use the deprecated `align` attribute within the table: `<table align="center">`. (Not all browsers handle this the same way, so check this markup in all of them!)

✔ Enclose the table in a `<div>` element and use the `text-align` property to center its contents: `div.mytable {text-align: center;}`. (Recommended.)

The `<div>` element is discussed further in Chapters 8 and 9.

Adding Spans

Spanning is one of the reasons tables may be useful when arranging elements in your Web page.

Spanning enables you to stretch items across multiple cells; you essentially tear down a cell wall. Whether you need to span rows or columns, you can use the concept of spanning to wrangle your table into almost any arrangement.

Spanning columns and rows takes careful planning. That planning should occur during the sketching phase (as we describe earlier in this chapter, in the section "Sketching Your Table").

To span cells, you add one of these attributes to the `<td>` (that is, cell) element:

✔ `colspan` extends a cell *horizontally* (across multiple *columns*).

✔ `rowspan` extends a cell *vertically* (across multiple *rows*).

Spanning cells works using only (X)HTML attributes; CSS doesn't provide equivalent functionality. That said, the `<div>` element lets you do just about anything without even using a table that you can do with spanning inside a table (and explains why it's become the preferred approach for professional page designers).

Column spans

To span columns, use the `colspan` attribute in the `<td>` element and set its value equal to the number of cells you wish to span. Here we set the spanning column background to blue, and make text white and extra bold so it matches the appearance of plain black text on a white background in the two cells below.

Figure 11-10 illustrates a cell that spans two columns.

In this example, a single blue cell in the first row spans the white cells in the two columns of the next row. You use the colspan attribute set to 2, as shown in the following markup, because the cell in the first row spans two columns:

```
<!DOCTYPE html PUBLIC "-//W3C//DTD XHTML 1.0 Transitional//EN"
      "http://www.w3.org/TR/xhtml1/DTD/xhtml1-transitional.dtd">
<html xmlns="http://www.w3.org/1999/xhtml">
<head>
    <title>Tables</title>
</head>
<body>
 <table border="2" width="430" align="center" cellpadding="20"
    type="text/css" style="font-family: Arial, sans-serif; font-size: 18pt;">
  <tr>
    <td width="430" colspan="2" align="center"
    type="text/css"
    style="background-color: blue; color: white; font-weight: bolder;">
    contents </td>
  </tr>
  <tr>
    <td width="230" align="center"> contents </td>
    <td width="200" align="center"> contents </td>
  </tr>
 </table>
</body>
</html>
```

Note in the preceding example, and in the next one, we use incline CSS code to keep the style information together with the table markup. In production markup, you'd want to put your CSS markup into an external style-sheet file.

After you add a colspan attribute

- ↙ Verify that you have the appropriate number of `<td>` cells in the first row. For example, if you define a cell to span two columns, you should have one less `<td>` in that row. If you use `colspan="3"`, there should be two fewer `<td>` cells in that row.

- ↙ Make sure that the other rows have the appropriate number of `<td>` cells. For example, if you define a cell to span two columns, the other rows in that table should have two `<td>` cells to fill out the two columns.

Row spans

You use the `rowspan` attribute with the `<td>` tag. Figure 11-11 illustrates a cell that spans two rows.

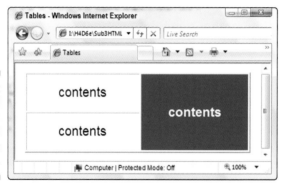

Figure 11-11:
The last cell
containing
navigational
items spans
two rows.

To span rows, you use the `rowspan` attribute in the `<td>` element and set the value equal to the number of cells you want to span.

Sketch your table first so you know which cells should span which columns and rows. The example design we use throughout most of this chapter uses the `colspan` attribute with the first cell. However, the design could have been just as simple if we used a `rowspan` with the last cell that contains the navigational items. Either way, the table is efficiently laid out.

The modified table comes from the following markup (note the bold `rowspan`):

```
<!DOCTYPE html PUBLIC "-//W3C//DTD XHTML 1.0 Transitional//EN"
    "http://www.w3.org/TR/xhtml11/DTD/xhtml1-transitional.dtd">
<html xmlns="http://www.w3.org/1999/xhtml">
<head>
    <title>Tables</title>
</head>
<body>
 <table border="2" width="430" align="center" cellpadding="20"
    type="text/css" style="font-family: Arial, sans-serif; font-size: 18pt;">
```

However, now you have a bit more flexibility to use CSS to add some color:

```
td {background-color: red;}
```

We cover the `background-color` property in Chapter 10.

The `bgcolor` attribute may be used with any of the table elements. However, the `bgcolor` of a cell overrides any `bgcolor` defined for a row or table. Note that `bgcolor` is also deprecated, and that most Web experts use CSS markup instead, using the aforementioned `background-color` property as well as the `color` property to set text or foreground color.

Other Table Markup of Interest

Table 11-1 lists other table-related (X)HTML attributes that you might find in HTML files.

Table 11-1   Additional Table-related (X)HTML Attributes

Name	Function/Value Equals	Value Types	Related Element(s)
`abbr`	Abbreviates table header cell name	Text	`<td> <th>`
`axis`	Sets a comma-separated list of related table headers	CDATA	`<td> <th>`
`char`	Defines alignment character for table elements	ISO 10646 char	`<col /> <colgroup> <tbody> <td> <tfoot> <th> <thead> <tr>`
`charoff`	Defines offset when alignment `char` is used	Length (p/%)	`<col /> <colgroup> <tbody> <td> <tfoot> <th> <thead> <tr>`
`frame`	Identifies visible components in a table structure	`{"above"|"below"|"border"|"box"| "hsides"|"lhs"|"rhs"|"void"|"vsides"}`	`<table>`
`rules`	Governs the display of rule bars in a table	`{"all"|"cols"|"groups"|"none"|"rows"}`	`<table>`
`scope`	Describes scope for table-header cells	`{"col"|"colgroup"|"row"|"rowgroup"}`	`<td><th>`
`summary`	Describes a table's purposes for rendering as speech	Text	`<table>`
`span`	Sets the number of table columns to which `col` attributes apply	Number	`<col />`

Figure 12-1:
A script
pops up a
dialog box
telling you
what you
did wrong.

The page URL doesn't change and another browser window doesn't open when you try to search on nothing. The page responds to what you do without sending a request back to the Web server for a new page. This is why the page is considered *dynamic*.

If you tried this trick without using a script (that is, without dynamic functionality), the browser would send the empty search string back to the Web server. Then the server would return a warning page reminding the user to enter a search term. All the work would be done on the Web server instead of in the Web browser. This would be slower (because the request must first go to the server, and then the server must transmit the warning page back to your browser) — which would feel much less fluid to the user. It's much better to just click a button on the page and have an alert pop up instantly to help the user.

In the following sections, we showcase three common ways in which JavaScript can be used in your Web pages.

Don't worry about the details of the JavaScript code in the following examples. Just focus on how JavaScript scripts can be pasted into your Web page and work alongside your HTML markup.

Arrange content dynamically

JavaScript can be used with CSS (covered in Chapters 8 and 9) to change the look of a page's content in response to a user action. Here's an example: Two authors share a Weblog, Backup Brain (www.backupbrain.com). One of the authors prefers small, sans-serif type, and the other one finds it easier to read larger, serif type. So the Weblog has buttons that change the look of the site to match each person's preference. Of course, the site's visitors can use the buttons to switch the look of the type, too, and the site remembers the visitor's choice for future visits by setting a *cookie* (a small preference file written to the user's computer). Figure 12-2 shows the two looks for the page.

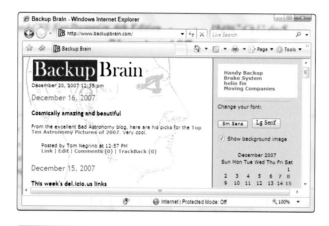

Figure 12-2: Clicking the "Change your font" buttons changes how the text displays.

JavaScript and CSS create this effect by switching between two style sheets:

- The sans-serif style sheet, `sansStyle.css`
- The serif style sheet, `serifStyle.css`

Listing 12-1 shows the source code for an example page that contains this switching mechanism.

- ✔ When a user clicks the Sm Sans button on the page, a script runs (styleSwitcher.js, referenced in the <head> element) and switches the active style sheet to sansStyle.css. (Chapter 13 covers .js files.)

- ✔ When the user clicks the Lg Serif button, the same script switches to the serifStyle.css style sheet.

Listing 12-1: Style Switching

```
<!DOCTYPE html PUBLIC "-//W3C//DTD XHTML 1.0 Transitional//EN"
        "http://www.w3.org/TR/xhtml1/DTD/xhtml1-transitional.dtd">
<html xmlns="http://www.w3.org/1999/xhtml">
<head>
    <title>Style Changer</title>
    <link href="simpleStyle.css" rel="stylesheet" rev="stylesheet" />
    <link href="sansStyle.css" rel="stylesheet" rev="stylesheet"
        title="default" />
    <link href="serifStyle.css" rel="alternate stylesheet"
        rev="alternate stylesheet" title="serif" />
    <style type="text/css" media="all">@import url("complexStyle.css");</style>
    <script src="styleSwitcher.js" language="javascript1.5"
        type="text/javascript"></script>
</head>
<body>
<div class="navBar">
<br />Change your font:
<form action="none">
    <input type="button" class="typeBtn" value="Sm Sans"
        onclick="setActiveStylesheet('default')" />
    <input type="button" class="typeBtn2" value="Lg Serif"
        onclick="setActiveStylesheet('serif')" />
</form>
</div>

<div class="content" id="headContent">
<p>Replace this paragraph with your own content.</p>
</div>
</body>
</html>
```

You can see the example page for yourself at

```
www.javascriptworld.com/chap11-3.html
```

This example relies on several different files (HTML, CSS, and JavaScript). You can download all 2.6 MB of these files if you'd like, from

```
www.javascriptworld.com/JavaScript6eScripts.zip
```

Work with browser windows

JavaScript can tell your browser to open and close windows.

You've probably seen an annoying version of this trick: advertising pop-up windows that appear when you try to leave a site. (Let's not go there.) But this technology can be used for good as well as evil. For example, you can preview a set of big image files with small thumbnail versions. Clicking a thumbnail image can perform such actions as

- ✔ Opening a window with a larger version of the image.

- ✔ Opening a page with a *text link* that opens a window with an illustration of that text, as shown in Figure 12-3.

Figure 12-3: When you click the link, a pop-up window appears with a picture in it.

The code required to do this sort of pop-up window is fairly straightforward, as Listing 12-2 shows.

Listing 12-2: Pop-up Windows

```
<!DOCTYPE html PUBLIC "-//W3C//DTD XHTML 1.0 Transitional//EN"
        "http://www.w3.org/TR/xhtml1/DTD/xhtml1-transitional.dtd">
<html xmlns="http://www.w3.org/1999/xhtml">
<head>
    <title>Opening a Window</title>
    <script language="Javascript" type="text/javascript">
```

```
    function newWindow() {
        catWindow = window.open("images/pixel2.jpg", "catWin",
          "width=330,height=250")
    }
    </script>
</head>
<body bgcolor="#FFFFFF">
    <h1>The Master of the House</h1>
    <h2>Click on His name to behold He Who Must Be Adored<br /><br />
    <a href="javascript:newWindow()">Pixel</a></h2>
</body>
</html>
```

Pop-up windows can backfire on you if you use them too much. Many Web sites use pop-up windows to deliver ads, so users are becoming desensitized (or hostile) to them, and simply ignore them (or install software that prevents them). Before you add a pop-up window to your site, be sure it's absolutely necessary.

Chapter 13 has more details on creating pop-up windows with JavaScript.

Solicit and verify user input

A common use for JavaScript is to verify that users have filled out all the required fields in a form before the browser actually submits the form to the form-processing program on the Web server. Listing 12-3 places a form-checking function, `checkSubmit`, in the `<script>` element of the HTML page and references it in the `onsubmit` attribute of the `<form>` element.

Listing 12-3:   Form Validation

```
<!DOCTYPE html PUBLIC "-//W3C//DTD XHTML 1.0 Transitional//EN"
        "http://www.w3.org/TR/xhtml1/DTD/xhtml1-transitional.dtd">
<html xmlns="http://www.w3.org/1999/xhtml">
<head>
  <title>Linking scripts to HTML pages</title>
  <script type="text/javascript" language="javascript">
    function checkSubmit ( thisForm ) {
      if ( thisForm.FirstName.value == '' ) {
            alert('Please enter your First Name.');
            return false;
      }

      if ( thisForm.LastName.value == '' ) {
            alert('Please enter your Last Name.');
            return false;
      }

      return true;
```

(continued)

Listing 12-3 *(continued)*

```
     }
   </script>
   </head>

   <body>
     <form method="POST" action="/cgi-bin/form_processor.cgi"
           onsubmit="return checkSubmit(this);">
     <p>
       First Name: <input type="text" name="FirstName" /><br />
       Last Name: <input type="text" name="LastName" /><br />
       <input type="submit" />
     </p>
     </form>
   </body>
   </html>
```

This script performs one of two operations if either form field isn't filled in when the user clicks the Submit button:

- ✔ It instructs the browser to display a warning to let the user know he or she forgot to fill in a field.

- ✔ It returns a value of `false` to the browser, which prevents the browser from actually submitting the form to the form-processing application.

If the fields are filled in correctly, the browser displays no alerts and returns a value of `true`, which tells the browser the form is ready for the Web server. Figure 12-4 shows how the browser displays an alert if the first name field is empty.

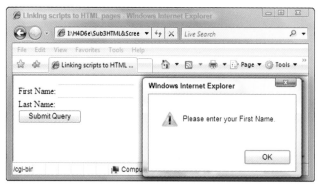

Figure 12-4: A good use of JavaScript is to validate form data.

Although this example only verifies whether users filled out the form fields, you can create more advanced scripts that check for specific data formats (such as @ signs in e-mail addresses and only numbers in phone number fields).

When you create forms that include required fields, we recommend that you always include JavaScript field validation to catch missing data before the script finds its way back to the server. Visitors get frustrated when they take the time to fill out a form only to be told to click the Back button to provide missing information. When you use JavaScript, the script catches any missing information before the form page disappears so users can quickly make changes and try to submit again.

But wait . . . there's more!

You can do much more with JavaScript. The following list highlights several common uses of the scripting language:

- Detect whether a user has a browser plug-in installed that handles multi-media content
- Build slide shows of images
- Automatically redirect the user to a different Web page
- Add conditional logic to your page, so that if the user performs a certain action, other actions are triggered
- Create, position, and scroll new browser windows
- Create navigation bars and change the menus on those bars dynamically
- Automatically put the current date and time on your page
- Combine JavaScript and CSS to animate page elements

Server-side scripting

JavaScript is a scripting language that runs inside the browser, but there are other scripting languages that run on the server side — such as Perl, ASP (Active Server Pages), PHP, Python, .NET, ColdFusion, and others. Programs written in these languages reside on the server and are called by the Web page, usually in response to a form filled out by the user. People who write these Web pages may include small snippets of code that pass bits of information from the HTML page to the program on the server. When

called, the program runs and then returns a result of some sort to the user.

Amazon.com is a familiar e-commerce Web application that runs mostly on the server side, using server scripts. Therefore Web pages displayed by the browser when you visit Amazon are the result of processing server-side scripts — all of which takes place before the page ever gets to your browser.

An innovative use of JavaScript occurs in Gmail, the free Web-based e-mail service from Google, which you can find at `www.gmail.com`. Gmail uses JavaScript to load an entire e-mail user interface into the user's browser, which makes Gmail much more responsive to user actions than most other Web-based mail programs. Gmail uses JavaScript to keep to an absolute minimum the number of times the page has to fetch additional information from the servers. By doing much of the processing in the user's browser, the Gmail Web application feels more like an e-mail program that runs on your computer. Figure 12-5 shows the JavaScript-powered Gmail interface. It's a great example of the power of JavaScript.

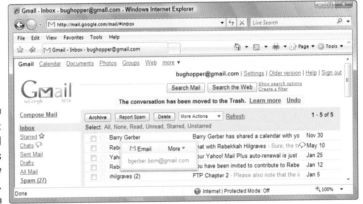

Figure 12-5:
The Gmail interface is powered by JavaScript.

Chapter 13

The Nuts and Bolts of JavaScript

A lot of good "canned JavaScript" is available for free on the Web; you know what we mean — scripts written by someone else that you simply copy and paste into your HTML page. But as good as canned scripts can be, copy-and-paste goes only so far. Sooner or later, you're going to encounter unique needs that can't be fulfilled with a free script.

Canned JavaScript is much like canned Spam (the meat product, not the e-mail affliction): Great for convenience, but you probably don't want to make it an exclusive diet. Instead, knowing how to script — or at least how to tweak a prewritten script — is as important as knowing how to fix some good ol' fashioned home cooking.

In this chapter, you "open the can" of the JavaScript language and have a look at what's inside. (Don't worry; you won't encounter any meaty pink substances along the way.) You discover how to plug scripts into your pages, how to bundle your scripts into external JavaScript files to save time and effort, and how the nuts and bolts of the JavaScript language work. Finally, at the end of this chapter, we point you to good sources of additional information about JavaScript. These will come in handy as your scripting needs advance.

Including Scripts in Web Pages

Because a JavaScript script is a totally separate animal from HTML markup, you have to contain this JavaScript beast inside an HTML container tag, `<script>` and `</script>`. You can put a script in one of two places on an HTML page:

- Within the `<head>` and `</head>` tags (this is called a *header script*)
- Within the `<body>` and `</body>` tags (this is called a *body script*)

Header scripts contain code that you either want processed before the page loads or else you want them available to be called by other scripts in your Web page. Body scripts are executed when the `<body>` tag is processed. Typically, body scripts are used to generate HTML content for the page.

Listing 13-1 shows a header script. This simple script pops up a welcoming message box when the user loads the page.

Listing 13-1: Header Script

```
<!DOCTYPE html PUBLIC "-//W3C//DTD XHTML 1.0 Transitional//EN"
      "http://www.w3.org/TR/xhtml1/DTD/xhtml1-transitional.dtd">
<html xmlns="http://www.w3.org/1999/xhtml">
<head>
   <title>My JavaScript page</title>
     <script language="Javascript" type="text/javascript">
       alert("Welcome to my JavaScript page!")
     </script>
</head>
<body bgcolor="#FFFFFF">
   <h2>This script pops up a message box for the user.</h2>
</body>
</html>
```

The preceding `<script>` tag has two attributes:

- `language="Javascript"` tells the browser which scripting language the document uses.
- `type="text/javascript"` tells the browser that the script is plain text in JavaScript.

The script itself, `alert("Welcome to my JavaScript page!")`, is straightforward. The `alert()` method displays a message box that pops up on top of the browser window and shows a customized message to the Web page visitor. You specify the message you want displayed by enclosing the text within quotation marks and putting the text string inside the `alert()` method's parentheses, as shown in Listing 13-1. (***Note:*** (Curly quotes and single quotes won't work.) Make sure you close the script with the `</script>` tag, and your script is ready to go.

Using the Same Script on Multiple Pages

If you have a single Web page that uses a JavaScript script, it's handy to be able to contain all the scripting code inside a single `<script>` tag. However, suppose you have a boatload of pages, each of which needs to call the same script. You can always copy and paste the script into each page, but there are two downsides to that approach:

 ✓ You have to add the script to each page and make sure it's set up correctly and working.

 ✓ Any time you tweak the script, you're forced to update *each and every HTML page that uses it.* If you have two pages, that's no big deal. But if you have more than three, it can lead to a maintenance migraine.

Fortunately, this latter headache can be avoided — even without ibuprofen! Instead, you can use an external JavaScript file, also called a `.js` file (pronounced "dot jay ess"). A `.js` file is an ordinary text file that stores your JavaScript scripts. You can store one or more of your JavaScript scripts in a single `.js` file and access them from multiple HTML pages. (It is much like the `.css` files in which you store external style sheets, except that a `.js` file stores external JavaScript code.)

To use the same script on multiple pages, you should

1. **Put the script in an external JavaScript file.**

   If you have the script already inside your HTML page, remove all the JavaScript code inside the `<script>` tag and paste it into a separate file.

2. **Reference the file in any HTML page when you need the script.**

   Define a `<script>` tag in the head section of your Web page, but don't add any code inside it. Instead, use the `src` (for *source*) attribute in the `<script>` tag to call the external `.js` file.

Listing 13-2 shows the reference to the external file.

Listing 13-2: External Script Reference

```
<!DOCTYPE html PUBLIC "-//W3C//DTD XHTML 1.0 Transitional//EN"
      "http://www.w3.org/TR/xhtml1/DTD/xhtml1-transitional.dtd">
<html xmlns="http://www.w3.org/1999/xhtml">
<head>
    <title>My JavaScript page</title>
<script src="external.js" language="JavaScript" type="text/javascript">
</script>
</head>
<!-- (the rest of your HTML page goes here) -->
```

You don't need to include anything else between the opening and closing script tags beyond what's shown. In Listing 13-2, the name of the source file, `external.js`, is placed between double quotes. You can reference this file, `external.js`, with either a relative or absolute link, so you can refer to external JavaScript files in other directories on your server, or even on other servers (if you have access to those servers).

Adding the `src` attribute to the `<script>` tag tells the browser to look for that external file in the specified path. The resulting Web pages look and act like the scripts are in the header or body of the page's script tags, though the script is in the external `.js` file.

With this technique, you need to change a JavaScript only once on your site in the external file, not in each individual page on the site. All pages that reference the external file automatically receive the updated code. It's a big time-saver when updating your site.

If you use a script on only one page, it's often easier simply to put the script on the page in a body or header script.

If you have multiple external `.js` files, you can use any or all of them on any HTML page. Just include multiple `<script>` references on the page. It's perfectly okay for a page to include multiple scripts — and to both refer to external `.js` files and to include its own scripts inside `<script>` tags.

When you have multiple `<script>` tags defined in your Web page, the browser processes them in the order in which they are declared. If, for some reason, you have an external `.js` file that conflicts with a script inside a `<script>` tag, the last one defined wins.

There is nothing magical about the inside of the `.js` file itself — it is pure JavaScript code. No HTML tags are allowed. Listing 13-3 shows an example of a script in an external `.js` file. This script implements button rollovers for a Web page. When the user moves the mouse pointer over a button image, the image changes to highlight the choice.

Figure 13-3:
An alert
pops up as
a result of
clicking the
H.G. Wells
button.

In the script, when the user clicks one of the buttons on the page, the say-Something function is called and is passed the information in quotes, which the function stores in the variable message. The function then displays the alert, with the value of message, which is the quotation it was passed.

Arrays

An *array* is a collection of values. Arrays are useful because you can use them to manipulate and sort groups of things.

The location of information in an array is based on a numbered position called the *index*. Index numbering always starts at 0 and goes up. JavaScript has a special object — the Array object — just to handle arrays.

Creating arrays

To create an instance of an array, you must use the new operator along with the Array object, like this:

```
x = new Array()
```

You can fill in the array when you create the Array object, separating the array elements with commas, like so:

```
theDays = new Array("Monday", "Tuesday", "Wednesday", "Thursday", "Friday",
                    "Saturday", "Sunday")
```

Accessing arrays

After the array is created, you can write to it and read from it by using the `[]` operator. By placing a position number in this operator, you can access the data stored at that index number.

For example, the value of `theDays[2]` in the preceding example is `Wednesday` (array positions always begin with 0, so `Monday` is 0). Please remember this, because many programming languages use 1 not 0 as their first array index value, and many new JavaScript programmers mistakenly think it works the same way.

Reading elements

To read an element from an array, create a variable and assign it a value from the array, like this:

```
thisDay = theDays[6]
```

The value of `thisDay` is now `Sunday`.

Writing elements

To write a value to the array, follow these steps:

1. Identify the index of the value you want to change.

2. Assign a new value to the array element, like this:

```
theDays[0] = "Mon"
```

Looping

Every array has a `length` property, which is very useful for discovering how many elements the array contains, and is often used to loop through the array elements, as in this example:

```
planets = new Array ("Mercury", "Venus", "Earth", "Mars")
for (i = 0; i < planets.length; i++)
alert (planets[i]);
```

This causes the browser to display a series of four alert boxes, each containing one of the names of the `planets` array. The value of `planets.length` is 3 (since numbering starts at 0), and the script steps through each element of the array until the value of the counting variable `i` is greater than 3, at which time the script ends.

Objects

Most JavaScript scripts are designed to "give life" to objects that exist inside your browser. A rollover brings an image link to life. A validated e-mail address field is smart about what kind of e-mail address it will accept. A document displays new text on the fly, basing what it shows on a response from the Web page visitor.

Within JavaScript, you work with a variety of objects — such as the browser window, a button, a form field, an image, or even the document itself. Because JavaScript's primary calling is to work with objects, the scripting language is called an *object-based language*.

Think, for a moment, of an object that exists in the real world, such as a car or an MP3 player. Each of these objects has characteristics that describe the object, such as color, weight, and height. Many objects also have a behavior that can be triggered. A car can be started; an MP3 player can be played.

These real-world analogies can be applied to JavaScript. Objects you work with have descriptive qualities (called *properties*) and behaviors (called *methods*). For example, a `document` object represents the HTML page in your browser. It has properties, such as `linkColor`, `title`, and `location`, as well as methods, such as `open()`, `clear()`, and `write()`. (JavaScript methods always have parentheses following their names.)

JavaScript uses periods (or dots) to access an object's properties or methods:

```
object.property
object.method()
```

For example, to get the `title` of the `document` and assign it to a variable, you write this:

```
mytitle = document.title
```

To call the `clear` method of the document, you write this:

```
document.clear()
```

Events and Event Handling

Events are actions that either the browser executes or the user performs while visiting your page. Loading a Web page, moving the mouse over an image, closing a window, and submitting a form are all examples of events.

JavaScript deals with events by using commands called *event handlers.* Any action by the user on the page triggers an event handler in your script. Table 13-6 is a list of JavaScript's event handlers.

Table 13-6	Event Handlers
Event Handler	**Description**
onabort	User cancels a page load.
onblur	An element loses focus (and is no longer available through the event handler) because the user focuses on a different element.
onchange	User changes the contents of a form element or selects a different check box, radio button, or menu item.
onclick	User clicks an element with the mouse.
ondblclick	User double-clicks an element with the mouse.
onerror	Browser encounters an error in the scripts or other instructions on the page.
onfocus	An element becomes the focus of the user's attention — as does (for example) a form field when you start typing in it.
onkeydown	User presses and holds a key on the keyboard.
onkeypress	User presses and immediately releases a key on the keyboard.
onkeyup	User releases a depressed key.
onload	Browser loads an HTML page.
onmouse-down	User moves the mouse pointer over an element, presses the mouse button down, and holds it down.
onmouse-move	User moves the mouse pointer anywhere on the page.
onmouseout	User moves the mouse pointer off an element.
onmou-seover	User moves the mouse pointer over an element.
onmouseup	User releases a held mouse button.
onreset	User clicks a form's Reset button.
onresize	User resizes the browser window.
onselect	User selects a check box, radio button, or menu item from a form.
onsubmit	User clicks a form's Submit button.
onunload	Browser stops displaying one Web page because it's about to load another.

Hidden fields

A *hidden field* gives you a way to collect name and value information that the user can't see along with the rest of the form data. Hidden fields are useful for keeping track of information associated with the form (such as its version or name).

If your Internet service provider (ISP) provides a generic application for a guest book or feedback form, you might have to put your name and e-mail address in the form's hidden fields so the data goes specifically to you.

To create a hidden field, you

✔ Use the `<input />` element with its `type` attribute set to `hidden`.

✔ Supply the name and value pair you want to send to the form handler.

Here's an example of markup for a hidden field:

```
<form action="cgi-bin/guestbook.cgi" action="post">
<input type="hidden" name="e-mail" value="me@mysite.com" />
<p>First Name: <input type="text" name="firstname" size="30"
                maxlength="25" /></p>
<p>Last Name: <input type="text" name="lastname" size="30" maxlength="25" /></p>
<p>Password: <input type="password" name="psswd" size="30" maxlength="25" /></p>
</form>
```

As a general rule, using your e-mail address in a hidden field is just asking for your address to be picked up by spammers. If your ISP says that this is how you should do your feedback form, ask them if they have any suggestions for how you can minimize the damage. Surfers to your page can't see your e-mail address, but spammers' spiders can read the underlying tags. At a minimum, you would hope that your ISP supports one of the many JavaScript encryption tools available to obscure e-mail addresses from harvesters.

File uploads

A form can receive documents and other files, such as images, from users. When the user submits the form, the browser grabs a copy of the file and sends it with the other form data. To create this *file-upload field,*

✔ Use the `<input />` element with the `type` attribute set to `file`.

The file itself is the form field value.

✔ Use the `name` attribute to give the control a name.

Here's an example of markup for a file-upload field:

```
<form action="cgi-bin/guestbook.cgi" action="post">
<p>Please submit your resume in Microsoft Word or plain text format:<br />
    <input type="file" name="resume" />
</p>
</form>
```

Browsers render a file-upload field with a browse button that allows a user to surf his or her local hard drive and select a file to send to you, as in Figure 14-9.

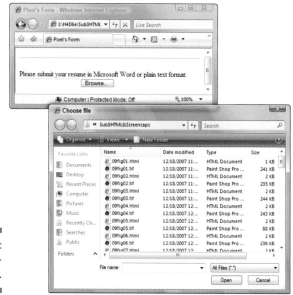

Figure 14-9:
A file-
upload field.

When you accept users' files through a form, you can receive files that are either huge or are infected by viruses. Consult with whoever is programming your form handler to discuss options for protecting the system where files are saved. Several barriers can help minimize your risks, including

- ✓ Virus-scanning software
- ✓ Restrictions on file size
- ✓ Restrictions on file type

Drop-down lists

Drop-down lists are a great way to give users lots of options in a little screen space. You use two different tags to create a drop-down list:

✔ `<select>` holds the list.

Use a `name` attribute with the `<select>` element to name the entire list.

✔ A collection of `<option>` elements identifies the list options.

The `value` attribute assigns a unique value for each `<option>` element.

Here's an example of markup for a drop-down list:

```
<form action="cgi-bin/guestbook.cgi" action="post">
<p>What is your favorite food?</p>
<select name="food">
  <option value="pizza">Pizza</option>
  <option value="icecream">Ice Cream</option>
  <option value="eggsham">Green Eggs and Ham</option>
</select>
</form>
```

The browser turns this markup into a drop-down list with three items, as shown in Figure 14-10.

Figure 14-10:
A drop-down list.

You can enable users to select more than one item from a drop-down list by changing the default settings of your list:

✔ If you want your user to be able to choose more than one option (by holding down the Alt [Windows] or ⌘ [Mac] key while clicking options in the list), add the `multiple` attribute to the `<select>` tag. The value of `multiple` is `multiple`.

Because of XHTML rules, standalone attributes cannot stand alone; therefore, the value is the same as the name of the attribute.

✔ By default, the browser displays only one option until the user clicks the drop-down menu's arrow to display the rest of the list. Use the `size` attribute with the `<select>` tag to specify how many options to show.

If you specify fewer than the total number of options, the browser includes a scroll bar with the drop-down list.

You can specify that one of the options in the drop-down list be already selected when the browser loads the page, just as you can specify a check box or radio button to be checked. Simply add the `selected` attribute to have a value of `selected` for the `<option>` tag you want as the default.

The following markup

✔ Allows the user to choose more than one option from the list

✔ Displays two options

✔ Selects the third option in the list by default

```
<form action="cgi-bin/guestbook.cgi" action="post">
<p>What are some of your favorite foods?</p>
<select name="food" size="2" multiple="multiple">
 <option value="pizza">Pizza</option>
 <option value="icecream">Ice Cream</option>
 <option value="eggsham" selected="selected">Green Eggs and Ham</option>
</select>
</form>
```

Figure 14-11 shows how adding these attributes modifies the appearance of the list in a browser.

Figure 14-11: A drop-down list with modifications.

```
      </script>
   </head>
   <body>
   The current time is <span id="myClock">?</span>
   </body>
   </html>
```

The script in Listing 15-5 is virtually identical to Listing 15-4, except for a couple of different lines of JavaScript. Using the DOM, the script can grab that text and replace it with new text every second.

  ✔ **The good news:** You can style that text with CSS and make it appear just like everything else on the page. The look is far superior to what you get if you put the dynamic text inside an `<input>` tag.

  ✔ **The bad news:** Older browsers don't support the `<span>` tag, so if your visitors use legacy versions of Netscape or Microsoft browsers, consider using the HTML and JavaScript version instead.

Other examples in this book show the initial `<script>` tag with the `lan-guage` attribute set to `javascript`. This particular script specifies `javascript1.5`, which tells the browser to ignore everything that's going on if you aren't using a modern browser. If you come into this page with an older browser, you won't get an error, but you won't get the dynamic effects, either.

To add the DOM-enabled scripted clock to your page, follow these steps:

  1. **Add everything between the beginning and ending** `<script>` **tags to the** `<head>` **section of your page.**

  2. **Add a** `<span>` **tag with an id attribute of** `myClock` **anywhere on your page.**

     The clock appears!

Are you getting errors when you try to add the DOM-powered clock to your page? Some browsers have a problem with either nothing or a space in the `<span>` tag. Solution: As with the example shown in Listing 15-5, put some-thing (anything) inside the `<span>` tag for when it's initially loaded. In this case, there's a question mark, but it won't ever be visible to Web page visitors.

Displaying Pop-up Windows

Pop-up windows can be useful, but they're also one of the most abused tools on the Web. Having a way to provide some extra information to site visi-tors without making them leave your page is useful. Unfortunately, so many unethical people have given pop-ups (in particular, advertising pop-ups) a bad name that many Web surfers install pop-up blockers. Consequently, if you add pop-up windows to your site, make sure that they aren't the only way visitors can access vital information.

Figure 15-7 shows a simple pop-up window containing the clock from Listing 15-5. This little window is a nice, floating, constantly updated clock that can stay up even after you've left the calling page. Listing 15-6 shows how to create this pop-up window, which is a new browser window with no address bar, menu bar, scroll bars, status bar, or toolbars, as shown in Figure 15-7.

Figure 15-7:
Clicking the link opens a new browser window.

Listing 15-6: Opening a New Browser Window

```
<!DOCTYPE html PUBLIC "-//W3C//DTD XHTML 1.0 Transitional//EN"
        "http://www.w3.org/TR/xhtml1/DTD/xhtml1-transitional.dtd">
<html xmlns="http://www.w3.org/1999/xhtml">
<head>
    <title>Window opener</title>
    <meta http-equiv="Content-Type" content="text/html; charset=ISO-8859-1" />
    <script type="text/javascript" language="javascript">
        function OpenWindow (newPage) {
            window.open(newPage,"newWin","width=200,height=50,resizable=yes");
        }
    </script>
</head>
<body>
<a href="domClock.html"
    onclick="OpenWindow(this.href);return false">Open a new clock</a>
</body>
</html>
```

The "Open a new clock" link, when clicked, calls a tiny JavaScript function that opens a new window that's 200 pixels wide, 50 pixels high, and resizable. You also need to rename the code from Listing 15-5 to `domClock.html` and save it into the same directory where Listing 15-6 lives.

Follow these steps to add this new window to your own site:

1. **Add everything from the beginning to the ending** `<script>` **tags to the** `<head>` **of your page.**

2. **In the body, figure out where you want the link to be.**

3. **Add the** `onclick` **event handler attribute to the** `<a href>` **tag around the text or image.**

You can have multiple links on the same page that each open a new window, and they can all have identical `onclick` handlers and call the same JavaScript function.

The script is coded so that all the different bars — address bars, menu bars, mini-bars, you name it — are turned off. You can change the code so the window sizes are different (or various fields either are or aren't displayed) by varying the contents of the last field in the `window.open` function. Table 15-1 shows the valid entries for this parameter: Just put them all, separated by commas (but not spaces), into a single string, and you get exactly the results you want.

The default for every JavaScript Window parameter is `no`, so there's no difference between setting an entry to `no` and just leaving it off entirely.

Table 15-1	JavaScript's Window Parameters	
Name	*Values (Default in Italics)*	*Description and Value*
`location`	yes, *no*	Should the new window display the location bar (also known as the address bar)?
`menubar`	yes, *no*	Should the new window display the menu bars? (Applies only to Windows and Unix.)
`resiz-able`	yes, *no*	Should the user be allowed to resize the new window?
`scroll-bars`	yes, *no*	Should the user be allowed to scroll the new window?
`status`	yes, *no*	Should the new window display the status bar?
`toolbar`	yes, *no*	Should the new window display the toolbar?

(continued)

Table 15-1 *(continued)*

Name	Values (Default in Italics)	Description and Value
`height`	Numeric	The height of the new window in pixels
`width`	Numeric	The width of the new window in pixels
`top`	Numeric	The top position of the new window in pixels, relative to the top edge of the browser window
`left`	Numeric	The left position of the new window in pixels, relative to the left edge of the browser window

Working with Cookies

Every time we start talking about cookies, we are tempted to grab a glass of milk and get ready for dipping. But then we remind ourselves that Web cookies, as useful as they can be, actually taste pretty bland. (We imagine they'd taste far more like chicken than the famous Toll House recipe.) Although they may not be tasty, you might find cookies to be helpful as you create your Web site.

A cookie lets you store information on visitors' computers that you can revisit later. Cookies offer a powerful way to maintain "state" within your Web pages.

The code in Listing 15-7 reads and writes two cookies when a visitor loads the page:

- ✔ `pageHit` contains a count of the number of times the visitor has loaded the page.
- ✔ `pageVisit` contains the last date and time the visitor visited.

Figure 15-8 shows how the page appears on the initial visit, and Figure 15-9 shows how it looks on subsequent visits.

```
<h1><img src="gregory-bbnt.jpg" alt="Gregory in the bluebonnets" width="180"
    height="240" align="middle" hspace="10" />Welcome to my home page!</h1>
<h2>About me:</h2>
<p>My name is Gregory. I'm a Montessori school student, and I'm interested
    in movies, music, bouncing, and sports. I love bacon and other kinds of
    meat, eat bread and fried polenta, and hate green vegetables.</p>
<h2>Sites I like:</h2>
<p>I'm a major Disney movie fan, so the
<a href="http://www.disneymovieslist.com/">
Disney Movie List</a> remains a source of constant inspiration</p>
<p>My enduring favorite is the Disney Pixar movie <i>Cars</i>, so the
<a href="http://cars.starsfansite.com/">Number #1 CARS movie fansite</a>
totally rocks.</p>
<h2>Send me email: <a href="mailto:gregory@edtittel.com">
    <img src="email.jpg" alt="email image" width="48" height="66"
    align="middle" border="0" /></a></h2>
</body></html>
```

This page is about as simple as it gets: There's no style information, no JavaScript, only two images, and not a lot of text. But it's enough to give you an idea of what kind of person put up the site and what he's like.

Figure 16-1:
A simple home page.

- `gregory-bbnt.jpg` is a favorite photo that shows the site subject in a field of Texas bluebonnets.
- `email.jpg` is a button that visitors can click. When a visitor clicks it, his or her e-mail client pops open in a window with a preaddressed e-mail.

It isn't hard to go from a super-simple site to a site that's considerably more attractive without getting horribly complex. Listing 16-2 and Figure 16-2 show a site with a lot more style and only a little more complexity.

Listing 16-2: Another Home Page

```
<!DOCTYPE html PUBLIC "-//W3C//DTD XHTML 1.0 Transitional//EN"
        "http://www.w3.org/TR/xhtml1/DTD/xhtml1-transitional.dtd">
<html xmlns="http://www.w3.org/1999/xhtml">
<head>
    <title>My Home Page</title>
    <meta http-equiv="Content-Type" content="text/html; charset=ISO-8859-1" />
    <style type="text/css">
        body {color: #000; background-color: #9C6;}
        h1 {font: 48px "monotype corsiva", fantasy;}
        h2 {margin-top: 20px; font: 20px "trebuchet ms", verdana,
            arial, helvetica, geneva, sans-serif;}
        p {margin-left: 20px; font: 14px/16px verdana, geneva, arial,
            helvetica, sans-serif}
    </style>
</head>
<body>
    <h1><img src="gregory-bbnt.jpg" alt="Gregory amidst bluebonnets" width="180"
            height="240"
        align="middle" hspace="10" />Welcome to my home page!</h1>
    <h2>About me:</h2>
    <p>My name is Gregory. I'm a Montessori school student, and I'm interested
        in movies, music, bouncing, and sports. I love bacon and other kinds of
        meat, eat bread and fried polenta, and hate green vegetables.</p>
    <h2>Sites I like:</h2>
    <p>I'm a major Disney movie fan, so the
    <a href="http://www.disneymovieslist.com/">
    Disney Movie List</a> remains a source of constant inspiration</p>
    <p>My enduring favorite is the Disney Pixar movie <i>Cars</i>, so the
    <a href="http://cars.starsfansite.com/">Number #1 CARS movie fansite</a>
    totally rocks.</p>
    <h2>Send me email: <a href="mailto:gregory@edtittel.com">
        <img src="email.jpg" alt="email image" width="48" height="66"
        align="middle" border="0" /></a></h2>
</body>
</html>
```

Text and tags within the <body> element are about the same as inside the first example, but the result is different because of the style rules in the <head>.

Figure 16-2:
Our less-
simple-and-
more-stylish
home page.

The style rules set a background color for the page and specify the fonts to be used. Although the two pages share identical content, the latter page gives a stronger impression of its maker's personality.

Looking good

Adding cool fonts and bright colors to your page is a good way to add visual interest — but it makes your site look tacky if it's overdone.

Follow these tips for a colorful, professional-looking page:

✏ **Pick a graphic and use its colors elsewhere on the page.**

The green at the back of the photo harmonizes nicely with the green background:

- The background color in the photo blends with the background color for the page (if you use transparent gifs and pick the same background color, it will blend in seamlessly).

- The color of the background also provides the color for the e-mail icon (we built it at `www.tomaweb.com`, using their free button gif builder).

✏ **Check your page on other computers to make sure your colors really look the way you want them to look.**

Colors often appear differently on different monitors, and not everyone's monitor is set up correctly.

✏ **Be selective when choosing fonts and font colors.**

- A font on your computer might not be on other computers.

  Provide alternate fonts as a backup in your style rules.

- Don't use too many different fonts on one page or it'll end up looking like a ransom note.

- Use font colors that contrast with your background so people can read what you've written.

Listing 16-3 is a bare-bones template with comments that tell you where to add your own content. Start with this, and where you end up is limited only by your imagination and creativity.

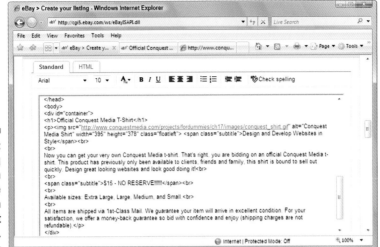

Figure 17-2:
Entering
HTML in
the online
description
form field at
eBay.

eBay allows you to use HTML for style only in the item description; you can't use it in the title or subtitle lines.

Because the auction site itself creates much of what appears on an online auction page, you don't have to create the entire page of HTML markup. You just create markup for the item-description part of the page. That means

✔ You don't need to include the `<html>`, `<title>`, `<head>`, or `<body>` tags (remember, your markup will be part of a larger, complete HTML document).

✔ You can't include any scripts in the description.

When you create your auction-item page, be aware that all browsers are not created equal. A couple of limitations apply:

✔ If you use Microsoft Internet Explorer 6 or newer as your browser, eBay gives you an HTML editor that allows you to style text directly — and then turns it into HTML markup, as shown in Figure 17-2 (notice the HTML tab above the text-entry box; we're using the Windows Vista IE version 7.0.6000).

✔ Other browsers, including Mozilla Firefox and Safari on the Macintosh, now also support tabs for Standard (plain text) or HTML (markup) which you can use the same way.

When designing your item's title and description, don't immediately rush to add fancy HTML formatting. Instead, your first task is to create a description that effectively presents your product. Before you worry about the HTML markup, write a compelling title and description. Consider the following tips when you write your text:

- **Write a concise, descriptive title.** A good title includes words that clearly and specifically identify what you are selling. eBay's search engine uses these titles to help people find your item, and you won't sell what buyers can't find.

- **Look at completed listings to see successful descriptions.** Use those ideas to stimulate your own.

  However, don't plagiarize other people's descriptions (or rip off their pictures). That way lies trouble.

- **Spell words in the title and description correctly.** Misspelled words won't be found by visitors searching for your item.

  In fact, we've bought equipment worth thousands of dollars for a fraction of its market value, largely because it got no other bids — all because the sellers misspelled the items' names in the auction titles.

- **Be sure that you're listing the item in the proper auction category.** If you list it in the wrong category, your item will get lost, buried, obscured, masked . . . well, you get the idea.

- **Resist the temptation to use large fonts and lots of styles.** Buyers want to see your item description and photographs as quickly as possible. Keep your text and images direct, visually uncluttered, and to the point.

- **Use good photographs or illustrations.** Items with pictures or graphics sell much better:

  - The photo of your item (more than one is usually better) should be sharp, with the item's important features clearly visible.

  - Make sure that your image files are a reasonable size; buyers hate large photos that take a long time to load or require scrolling (we recommend reducing photos to no larger than 640×480 pixels).

    Use a photo-editing program to reduce the pictures that your digital camera or scanner produces to a smaller size and save them as lower-resolution JPEG files. You want a size that loads quickly and can be viewed without scrolling, as discussed in Chapter 7.

- **Avoid animation and music like the plague.** Serious bidders click off of your item in a flash if they find either of these annoyances in your item description.

Presentation Issues to Consider

When you create your listings, remember that a variety of users will view your page using different browsers and operating systems. With that in mind, peruse the following helpful tips for creating your listing:

- ✔ **Design your page so it works with as many browsers as possible.** Any Web browser may view your listing. (For example, you can't assume that your buyers have a browser capable of properly rendering CSS.)

- ✔ **Use an appropriate font size.** The font size that you use should be large enough to be legible at a variety of screen resolutions. Standard font sizes such as a 10- to 12-point font are good examples. Some buyers won't bother to read your item description if it is in a tiny font size. At the same time, don't make the font size too large. Large fonts can make your auction item page look amateurish.

- ✔ **Don't use huge type that requires users to scroll the page a lot.** For example, four headings—all in a 48-point font—is way too big.

- ✔ **Use backgrounds that don't distract your users from the text and images on the Web site.**

    Avoid colored or patterned backgrounds because

    - People who are colorblind might have problems reading them.

    - Colored backgrounds can make your page hard to read when printed on a monochrome printer. (Many users print auctions for inventory records.)

    - They can make your page look amateurish.

Using a Template for Presenting Your Auction Item

In this section, we provide a handy HTML template that enables you to display pictures of your item alongside its description:

- ✔ **A left column contains two pictures of the auction item.**

    The example assumes that you're hosting the image files on a Web server that you control. (Though eBay will now let you host one image per auction for free, you must pay for additional images; if you don't mind spending money on this, feel free to upload them using the eBay auction setup form instead.) You should prepare the image files and upload them to your server before you begin using the template.

- ✔ **A right column contains text describing the item.**

Listing 17-1 shows the HTML markup for the auction item description. You can type it in any text editor, replacing the parts set off by the HTML comment tags with the appropriate information (as indicated in the comment-tag text).

Listing 17-1: Auction Item HTML Template

```
<!-- Begin Description Table -->
<!-- Picture column -->

<table align="center" cellpadding="8" border="7"
      cellspacing="0" bgcolor="#FFFFFF">
<tr>
<td valign="top" align="Left" width="1%"><br /><br />

<!-- First picture goes below; replace URL with the location of your picture -->

<img border="0" align="top" hspace="5"
     src="http://www.example.com/images/image1.jpg"
     alt="Alternative image text" />

<br /><br />

<!-- Next picture goes below; replace URL with the location of your picture -->

<img border="0" align="top" hspace="5"
     src="http://www.example.com/images/image1.jpg"
     alt="Alternative image text" /></td>

<!-- Text column -->

<td valign="top" align="Left">

<!-- This table-within-a-table for the headline makes your description
     look better -->

<table border="0" >
  <tr><td align="Left" ><font face="Times New Roman" color="#000000" size="6">
     Your Exciting Item Title Goes Here!</font>
  </td></tr>
</table><br />

<p><font face="Times New Roman" color="#000000" size="3">

<!-- Begin Description -->

Replace this text with the description of your auction item.

<!-- End Description -->

</font></p>

<p><font face="Times New Roman" color="#000000" size="2">
```

```
<!-- Enter your payment terms and details here. -->

  </font></p>

<p><font face="Times New Roman" color="#000000" size="2">

<!-- Enter your shipping terms and details here. -->

  </font></p>

  </td>
  </tr>
</table>

  <!-- End Description Table -->
```

In Figure 17-3, you can see the on-screen results of the preceding auction item-description template. (We sold many copies of this item successfully on eBay.)

Figure 17-3: The template as it appeared on eBay.

Many auction sites, including eBay, host pictures for your item — often for free. For example, eBay hosts one picture for free, but you must pay for extra pictures. You might also consider using sites such as Picasa (http://picasa.google.com) that offer free image-hosting services that include Web access for online auction sellers.

Chapter 18

A Company Site

Companies large and small differ on their office dress policies — from being required to wear three-piece suits in the office to being allowed to work in a SpongeBob T-shirt and torn cutoffs. However, all companies, despite their differences in formality and workwear, want to present themselves effectively to the outside world. As such, they want their Web sites to reek of confidence, capability, and professionalism. No one feels good about forking over hard-earned money to a company with a cheesy and tacky Web site (unless that company sells cheese and tacks).

In this chapter, you explore the basics of creating a company Web site — and look at the typical elements you want to utilize as you design your own company's site.

Issues to Consider When Designing Your Site

When you start to plan your company's Web site, the most important task is to consider the kind of people who are going to visit — potential or existing customers, clients, or partners. After you determine a list of the types of visitors, brainstorm about what they will want from your Web site.

Working with the concept of *personas* (okay, that's *personae* in Latin), in which you envision a few of the site's visitors and what they each want to get from the site, can be valuable. As you lay out the site, think about how each of these imaginary people interacts with your design. Will they find what they're looking for?

If you're designing a site for a company that has many departments, you'll soon discover that each department may have a different vision of what the company Web site should be. For instance, marketing wants the front page of the site to be a gigantic Flash animation showing all the company's products — whereas management wants every page on the site to look exactly like a corporate brochure and to look the same in every browser known to humankind.

Your job, as a Web designer and developer, is not only to design the site but also to educate people around you about what is possible and feasible — while staying within your budget.

Basic Elements of a Company Web Site

As you consider creating a company Web site, consider the following among basic elements that you may want to include. As a purely hypothetical but hopefully illustrative example, this sample company site includes six key files:

- ✔ **The initial Web page,** `index.html`, is the site's home page. It contains the basic marketing message about the company and its services; despite its name, it's entitled "About Us." For most company Web sites, the home page presents key facts about the company and identifies its business focus, target markets, and seeks to attract visitors to explore further.

  A site's home page can have any of a variety of file names, such as `index.html`, `default.html`, and `home.html`. You want to check with your Webmaster or your Web-hosting provider to determine the exact filename you should use. However, in general, the filename `index.html` will almost always work.

- ✔ **The products/services pages** are named `multimedia.html`, `print.html` and `web_design.html`. Each contains summary information about company projects and services, related to multimedia and print projects, as well as custom Web-design services. When creating filenames, keep them short, simple, and intelligible so you and others can at least guess what they hold.

- ✔ **The contact us page,** `contactus.html`, contains an e-mail link to the company to enable visitors to communicate with the principals via e-mail. Let's also observe again that it's essential to respond rapidly, professionally, and thoroughly to such inquiries. Many "Contact Us" pages also include a mail address and one or more phone numbers for the company; some even include (or point to) maps and directions to reach company HQ or other locations.

✔ **A press page,** `press.html`, contains

- Links to the press releases generated by the company

- Information that marketing thinks members of the press might want, such as news coverage, analyst reports, product reviews, and even image libraries (if applicable)

This page isn't discussed in the rest of the chapter, but you can easily modify the basic HTML template discussed for the other site pages to create this unique page on your own.

✔ **An image,** `logo.gif`, is displayed on the site's home page to give visitors an initial impression of the company and its creative ethos. This could be any image, from a company logo to pictures of employees in action. On our sample site, we repeat this same image at the head of each page on the site. This is a common technique, and helps to establish a sense of continuity and branding to help hold your site together.

✔ **A style sheet,** `style.css`, contains the formatting instructions for each page of the site.

Every page links to this style sheet by using the `<link>` tag. A change in this file changes the appearance of every page on the site.

The home page

Listing 18-1 shows the home-page markup for Conquest Media, our not-so-fictitious company (it represents author Jeff Noble's growing business venture). Figure 18-1 shows how it looks when displayed in a browser.

Listing 18-1:   Our Company's Home Page (index.html)

```
<!DOCTYPE html PUBLIC "-//W3C//DTD XHTML 1.0 Transitional//EN"
    "http://www.w3.org/TR/xhtml1/DTD/xhtml1-transitional.dtd">
<html xmlns="http://www.w3.org/1999/xhtml">
<head>
  <meta http-equiv="Content-Type" content="text/html; charset=iso-8859-1">
  <title>Conquest Media</title>
  <link href="style.css" rel="stylesheet" type="text/css">
</head>
<body>
<!-- Main text area for body copy-->
  <div align="center"><img src="images/logo.gif" /></div>
<!-- Page container that centers contents  -->
  <div id="container">
<!-- Navigation  -->
  <div id="nav">
```

(continued)

Listing 18-1 *(continued)*

```
<ul>
  <li><a href="index.html">[about us]</a></li>
  <li><a href="web_design.html">[web design]</a></li>
  <li><a href="multimedia.html">[multimedia]</a></li>
  <li><a href="print.html">[print]</a></li>
  <li><a href="contactus.html">[contact us] </a></li>
</ul>
</div> <!-- close nav division -->
<div id="container">
<h1>About Us</h1>
<p>Conquest Media is an Austin multimedia company providing a
   variety of design solutions for clients within Austin,
   Houston, Dallas/Ft. Worth areas of Texas, across the United
   States and around the world. We specialize in creating
   cutting edge web designs, dynamic multimedia, and print
   design solutions to suit all business needs.</p>
<p>We understand that every client of Conquest Media has
   different requests and specifications that we will gladly meet.
   It&rsquo;s our guarantee to work with you on a one-to-one basis
   to complete your project.</p>
<p>Our talented team of 3D artists, web designers, multimedia
   specialists, and database programmers has the experience, talent,
   technical knowledge and skills to deliver impressive and effective
   results. Simply put, there are a lot of design studios out there,
   and anyone can say they are a designer, but we have the portfolio
   to back it up. </p>
<p>We invite you to review our portfolio of web design, multimedia,
   and print designs to see just exactly what we do here, why we love
   it, and why people love our work.</p>
<div id="footer">All images and content &copy; Conquest Media 2008.
   All Rights Reserved.</div>
<!-- end #container --></div>
</body>
</html>
```

As you look at the markup in Listing 18-1, you can see that it doesn't contain any information about colors, fonts, or how the page itself should be displayed. All that information is *in the style sheet,* which allows the most flexible approach to updating the site in the future.

The navigation used in the home page and for the other site pages is based on a simple text bar (a collection of text links, each enclosed in square brackets [ ]). These links are simple, easy to code, and can be *spidered* (automatically searched for keywords) by search engines such as Google. They work as well in older browsers as they do in newer ones.

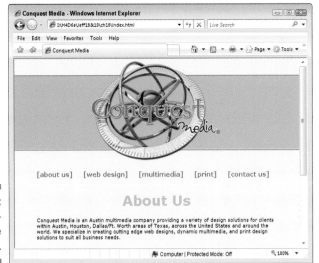

Figure 18-1:
Our com-
pany's home
page.

If you want to use this template for your home page, just

✔ Change the contents of the `<title>` and `<h1>` tags, and customize the navigation to meet your needs (you can use the text rollovers for navigation described in Chapter 15 instead, if you prefer).

✔ Add the company's description where text that follows the `<h1>` element occurs, after deleting the Conquest Media description.

It's all greeked to me

If you would like to mock up a page for which you don't yet have actual content, we recommend using greeked text. *Greeked text* is placeholder text that typically starts with the Latin phrase "Lorem Ipsum" and gets repetitively nonsensical from there. It's easy to tell apart from real text.

If you want to add greeked text to your page, check out `www.lipsum.com`, which will let you choose such options as the number of words, paragraphs, and bytes of greeked text you need. Then you can copy and paste the place holder text into your page.

The Web Design page

Listing 18-2 and Figure 18-2 show the company's Web Design page and demonstrate how the overall look is the same, yet slightly different, for an interior site page.

Listing 18-2:   Our Company's Web Design Page (web_design.html)

```
<!DOCTYPE html PUBLIC "-//W3C//DTD XHTML 1.0 Transitional//EN"
    "http://www.w3.org/TR/xhtml1/DTD/xhtml1-transitional.dtd">
<html xmlns="http://www.w3.org/1999/xhtml">
<head>
  <title>Conquest Media</title>
  <link href="style.css" rel="stylesheet" type="text/css">
</head>
<body>
  <div id="header"><img src="images/logo.gif" /></div>
<!-- Page container that centers contents  -->
  <div id="container">
  <div id="nav">
  <ul>
    <li><a href="index.html">[about us]</a></li>
    <li><a href="web_design.html">[web design]</a></li>
    <li><a href="multimedia.html">[multimedia]</a></li>
    <li><a href="print.html">[print]</a></li>
    <li><a href="contactus.html">[contact us]</a></li>
  </ul>
  </div> <!-- end navigation area -->
<h1>Web Design </h1>
  <div id="item">
  <div id="leftColumn">
    <img src="images/portfolio_web-1.gif"  alt="Arclight Records"
    width="190" height="146">
  </div> <!-- end leftColumn -->
  <div id="rightColumn">
  <p>Arclight Records wanted a unique website to showcase their
    rapidly growing record label. We provided a brand new creative
    look and integrated an existing online store where they sell
    their products.</p>
  <p><a href="http://www.arclightrecords.com">
    Click Here To View Website</a></p>
  </div><!-- end rightColumn -->
  </div> <!-- end Arclight item -->
  <div id="item">
  <div id="leftColumn">
  <img src="images/portfolio_web-2.gif" alt="Amy Komar"
   width="190" height="146">
  </div> <!-- end leftColumn -->
  <div id="rightColumn">
```

```
<p>Celebrated acrylic painter Amy Komar selected us from numerous
    design submissions. We created a custom design to emphasize her
    colorful paintings and administration section for her to update
    the site without any HTML knowledge.</p>
<p><a href="http://www.amykomar.com">
    Click Here To View Website</a></p>
</div> <!-- end rightColumn -->
</div> <!-- end Amy Komaritem -->
<div id="footer">All images and content &copy; Conquest Media 2008.
    All Rights Reserved.
</div> <!-- end footer -->
</div> <!-- end container -->
</body>
</html>
```

Figure 18-2: Our company's Web Design page.

To use the template shown in Listing 18-2, follow these steps:

1. **Customize the title, heading, footer, and navigation bar for your page.**

2. **Add descriptive text within the <p> tag to describe your products.**

3. **If it makes sense to do so, create a bulleted or numbered list (<ul> or <ol>), and describe each product specifically within individual <li> tags instead of using paragraphs of text.**

You can add links to subpages from within the individual product descriptions. If you do this, use this page as a template for the individual product pages, but make sure to create a Products link in the navigation bar. That way, site visitors can retrace their steps back to where they came from without clicking the Back button.

The Contact Us page

This simple page allows visitors to the site to send their feedback directly to the company. It provides an e-mail link, as shown in Listing 18-3 and Figure 18-3.

Listing 18-3:   Contact Our Company (contact.html)

```
<!DOCTYPE html PUBLIC "-//W3C//DTD XHTML 1.0 Transitional//EN"
    "http://www.w3.org/TR/xhtml1/DTD/xhtml1-transitional.dtd">
<html xmlns="http://www.w3.org/1999/xhtml">
<head>
<title>Conquest Media</title>
<link href="style.css" rel="stylesheet" type="text/css">
</head>
<body>
<!-- Main text area for body copy-->
<div id="header"><img src="images/logo.gif" /></div>
<!-- Page container that centers contents  -->
<div align="center">
<!-- Navigation  -->
<div id="nav">
<ul>
<li><a href="index.html">[about us]</a></li>
<li><a href="web_design.html">[web design]</a></li>
<li><a href="multimedia.html">[multimedia]</a></li>
<li><a href="print.html">[print]</a></li>
<li><a href="contactus.html">[contact us]</a></li>
</ul>
</div>
<div id="container">
<h1>Contact Us</h1>
  <p>We care about what you think about our site, our work, and our
     company. If you have a comment, question, or you want to request
     information, please contact us with the information below.</p>
<p><a href="mailto:info@conquestmedia.com">
info@conquestmedia.com</a></p>
<div id="footer">All images and content &copy; Conquest Media 2008.
    All Rights Reserved.</div>
<!-- end #container --></div>
<!-- end centered page> </div>
</body>
</html>
```

This chapter's example of a product catalog uses the following resources:

- Two templates for the product catalog:
  - A category page with small images of items within that category
  - A detail page for one example item

- The navigational menu system

Figure 19-1 shows the single category page for Conquest Media. Site visitors click the thumbnail picture of an item to jump to the detail page.

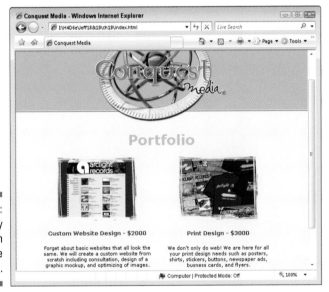

Figure 19-1:
A category
page from
the online
catalog.

After a visitor clicks an item in the category page, the item-detail page appears, as shown in Figure 19-2. This page contains the all-important Buy Now button, which allows the visitor to purchase the item.

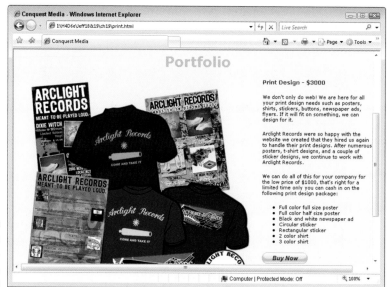

Choosing a Shopping Cart

If you want people to purchase from your site, you need a *shopping cart.* The cart allows buyers to purchase items and pay for them (usually with a credit card or a bank account transaction).

The shopping-cart software (which runs on a Web server) leads the buyer through the following steps of buying a product online:

1. The buyer selects an item and adds it to the shopping cart.

2. If the buyer wants to shop for other items, he or she can continue shopping and place other items in the shopping cart.

3. When ready to purchase, the buyer chooses to move to the *checkout* process.

   At checkout, the shopping cart software

   • Totals the purchases

   • Adds shipping costs (if necessary)

   • Leads the buyer through the payment process of entering such details as a credit card number and shipping address

In concept, a shopping cart for an online store is fairly simple. But in execution, it can get complex. This chapter surveys only the basics of e-commerce. If you are going to dive into it fully, we recommend these books:

✔ *Starting an Online Business For Dummies,* 5th Edition, by Greg Holden (Wiley)

✔ *MySQL/PHP Database Applications* by Brad Bulger, Jay Greenspan, and David Wall (Wiley)

PayPal

In this chapter, we use the shopping cart from a well-known e-commerce site, PayPal. Owned by eBay, PayPal's shopping cart is free for you to use on your Web site. Your customers can purchase multiple items with a single payment, and you can accept credit-card and bank-account payments. (PayPal charges you a transaction fee when you receive payment.)

PayPal offers a button generator that takes information about the name and price of an item you have for sale and creates HTML markup for an Add to Cart button that you can then insert directly into your product-catalog page.

This button generator and the PayPal shopping cart require a PayPal Premier or Merchant account. (PayPal Personal accounts don't accept debit- or credit-card payments; they only send or receive bank transfers.)

Other e-commerce solutions

PayPal is one of the easiest shopping carts to implement on your site, but many others are available.

The following technologies require more of a serious business and financial commitment to setting up your online presence.

Hosting e-commerce services

Hosted e-commerce services let you build an online storefront on your site but let the service provider deal with the technical aspects of your store and your transaction processing.

A good example of the online storefront service is Yahoo! Merchant Solutions (http://smallbusiness.yahoo.com/ecommerce). You can create a storefront on a Yahoo! server that features your own domain name, a product catalog, site-building tools (you can even avoid using raw HTML if you prefer), a secure shopping cart, e-mail order confirmations, integration with UPS for shipping, and order statistics tools. An online store on Yahoo! is fairly easy to set up and operate, especially if you're more merchant than Web developer. Prices start at about $40 a month.

Do-it-yourself software

If you are really a technical guru (or aren't faint of heart), you can install shopping-cart software on your own Web server and configure it manually.

If you choose this option, you need the technical know-how, a Web server, and a constant Internet connection for hosting your e-commerce Web site.

One do-it-yourself shopping cart software package is Zen Cart (`www.zen-cart.com`). It's a free, open-source shopping cart written in PHP. Stores created with Zen Cart are highly customizable with many useful features — for example, customers can review your products and you can customize tax and shipping rates for everywhere you sell your items.

If you use Zen Cart, expect to spend at least a few days setting up your store before you're ready for business. You must know how to upload and install Zen Cart software on your server, how to rename files and set UNIX permissions, and how to create a MySQL database. Then you must create or modify page templates for your store and supply numerous server-side parameters.

In general, we recommend you stick with PayPal or a hosted e-commerce solution to avoid the complexity of trying to do it all yourself. Don't say we didn't warn you!

Incorporating a PayPal shopping cart

Creating HTML markup for the shopping cart is easy: Use the PayPal button generator, and then copy and paste the resulting markup into your Web page.

To use a PayPal shopping cart, you must be a PayPal Premier or Merchant account holder. After you establish an account, you can create your own Add to Cart and View Cart (or Buy Now) buttons by performing the instructions shown in the following sections.

Add to Cart button

Follow these steps to insert an Add to Cart button on your page:

1. **In your Web browser, go to the PayPal site:** `https://www.paypal.com`.

   This site is secure, so all transactions are encrypted between the site and your browser.

2. **Log in to your Premier or Merchant account.**

   Your account overview appears, with details only you need to know about.

3. **Click the Merchant Tools tab.**

4. **On the Merchant Tools page, click the PayPal Shopping Cart link.**

5. **On the PayPal Shopping Cart page, fill out the information about the item you want to sell.**

   You must enter the item name, the price, and the currency you accept. An item number (used in reports that PayPal provides for you after the sale) and the default country for the buyer's payment form are optional.

6. **In the Select an Add to Cart Button section, click to select the button style shown.**

   If you don't like the style that appears in response, click the Choose a Different Button link to pick a different button style.

   You can *create* a button image and use it with the PayPal shopping cart:

   a. Create the button graphic in an image-editing program.

   b. Upload the graphic to a Web server.

   c. Select the Yes, I Would Like to Use My Own Image radio button on the PayPal Shopping Cart page.

   d. Fill in the URL for the graphic on your Web server.

7. **Click the Create Button Now button at the bottom of the page.**

8. **On the Add a Button to Your Website page, select *all* the text in the Add to Cart Button Code field, as shown in Figure 19-3, and then choose Edit➪Copy in your browser.**

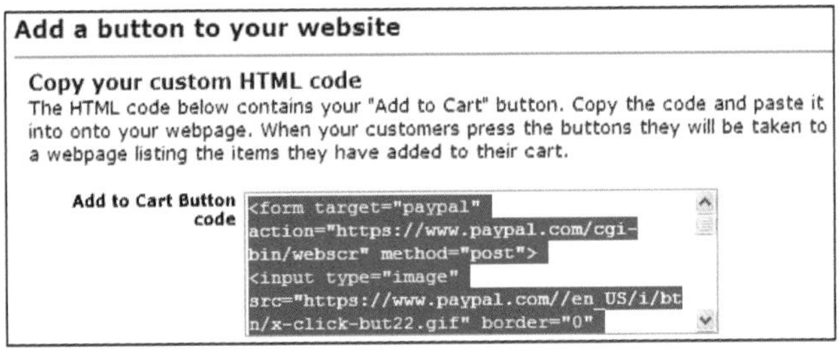

Figure 19-3:
Copying the
Add to Cart
button code.

Add a button to your website

Copy your custom HTML code
The HTML code below contains your "Add to Cart" button. Copy the code and paste it into onto your webpage. When your customers press the buttons they will be taken to a webpage listing the items they have added to their cart.

Add to Cart Button code

```
<form target="paypal"
action="https://www.paypal.com/cgi-
bin/webscr" method="post">
<input type="image"
src="https://www.paypal.com//en_US/i/bt
n/x-click-but22.gif" border="0"
```

9. **Switch to your HTML page editor and paste the cart code where you want the button to appear.**

10. **Save and preview the HTML page you just modified in your Web browser to see the button on the page.**

View Cart button

If you add a View Cart button to your page, follow these steps:

1. **Go to the PayPal Add a Button to Your Website page.**

   This HTML markup was generated at the same time as the Add a Button HTML markup.

2. **Select** *all* **the text in the View Cart Button Code field.**

3. **Copy and paste the code into your HTML page.**

Page Markup

Listing 19-1 includes the markup for the category page.

Listing 19-1: Category Page Template

```
<!DOCTYPE html PUBLIC "-//W3C//DTD XHTML 1.0 Transitional//EN"
http://www.w3.org/TR/xhtml1/DTD/xhtml1-transitional.dtd>
<html xmlns="http://www.w3.org/1999/xhtml">
<head>
<meta http-equiv="Content-Type" content="text/html; charset=utf-8" />
<title>Conquest Media</title>
<link href="style.css" rel="stylesheet" type="text/css">
<!-- See sample Web site at www.edtittel.com/html4d6e/ch19 for stylesheet -->
</head>
<body>
<div id="header"><img src="images/logo.gif" /></div>
<div id="container">
  <div id="mainContent">
    <h1>Portfolio</h1>
      <div id="leftColumn"><img src="images/portfolio_web-1.gif"
        alt="Website Design" width="190" height="146" />
      <p class="portfolio_text">Custom Website Design - $2000</p>
      <p>Forget about basic websites that all look the same. We will create a
        custom website from scratch including consultation, design of a
        graphic mockup, and optimizing of images.</p>
      </div> <!-- end left column markup -->
      <div id="rightColumn">
      <p><a href="print.html"><img src="images/porfolio_print-1.gif"
        alt="Print" width="190" height="147" border="0"></a>
      <p class="portfolio_text">Print Design - $3000</p>
      <p>We don't only do web! We are here for all your print design needs such
        as posters, shirts, stickers, buttons, newspaper ads, busness cards,
        and flyers.</p>
      </div> <!-- end right column markup -->
      <div id="footer">All images and content &copy; Conquest Media 2008.
        All Rights Reserved.</div>
```

```
    <!-- end #mainContent --></div>
  <!-- end #container --></div>
</body>
</html>
```

Listing 19-2 includes the markup for the detail-page template.

Listing 19-2:   Detail-Page Template

```
<!DOCTYPE html PUBLIC "-//W3C//DTD XHTML 1.0 Transitional//EN"
  "http://www.w3.org/TR/xhtml1/DTD/xhtml1-transitional.dtd">
<html xmlns="http://www.w3.org/1999/xhtml">
  <head>
  <meta http-equiv="Content-Type" content="text/html; charset=utf-8" />
  <title>Conquest Media</title>
  <link href="style.css" rel="stylesheet" type="text/css">
<!-- See sample Web site at www.edtittel.com/html14d6e/ch19 for stylesheet -->
</head>
<body>
  <div id="header"><img src="images/logo.gif" /></div>
  <div id="containerPrint">
    <div id="mainContent">
    <h1>Portfolio</h1>
    <div id="leftColumnPrint">
    <img src="images/porfolio_print-1.jpg" alt="Website Design"
     width="565" height="500" />
    </div> <!-- end leftColumnPrint markup -->
    <div id="rightColumnPrint">
    <p class="portfolio_text">Print Design - $3000</p>
    <p>We don't only do web! We are here for all your print design needs
        such as posters, shirts, stickers, buttons, newspaper ads, flyers.
        If it will fit on something, we can design for it. </p>
    <p>Arclight Records were so happy with the website we created that they
        hired us again to handle their print designs. After numerous posters,
        t-shirt designs, and a couple of sticker designs, we continue to work
        with Arclight Records.</p>
    <p>We can do all of this for your company for the low price of $1000,
        that's right for a limited time only you can cash in on the following
        print design package:</p>
    <!-- list of items-->
    <ul class="disc">
      <li>Full-color full-size poster </li>
      <li>Full-color half-size poster</li>
      <li>Black-and-white newspaper ad</li>
      <li>Circular sticker</li>
      <li>Rectangular sticker</li>
      <li>2-color shirt</li>
      <li>3-color shirt</li>
    </ul>
<!-- Paypal Button-->
```

(continued)

Listing 19-2 *(continued)*

```
<form action="https://www.paypal.com/cgi-bin/webscr" method="post">
<input type="hidden" name="cmd" value="_s-xclick" />
<input type="image"
 src="https://www.paypal.com/en_US/i/btn/btn_buynow_LG.gif" border="0"
 name="submit"
 alt="Make payments with PayPal - it's fast, free and secure!" />
<img alt="" border="0" src="https://www.paypal.com/en_US/i/scr/pixel.gif"
 width="1" height="1" />
<input type="hidden" name="encrypted" value="-----BEGIN PKCS7-----
    your PayPal security code here (you'll grab this when you cut'n'paste)
    -----END PKCS7-----" />
    </form>
</div> <!-- end rightColumnPrint markup -->
<div id="footer">All images and content &copy; Conquest Media 2008.
   All Rights Reserved.</div>
 </div> <!-- end #mainContent -->
</div> <!-- end #container -->
</body>
</html>
```

Check Your Site, and Then Check It Again!

There's an ongoing need for quality control in any kind of public content, but that need is particularly acute on the Web, where the whole world can stop by (and where success often follows the numbers of those who drop in *and return*). You must check your work while you're building the site and continue to check your work over time. This practice forces you to revisit your material with new and shifting perspectives, and to evaluate what's new and what's changed in the world around you. That's why testing and checking are never really over; they just come and go — preferably, on a regular schedule!

Look for trouble in all the right places

You and a limited group of hand-picked users should thoroughly test your site before you share it with the rest of the world — and more than once. This process is called *beta-testing,* and it's a bona fide, five-star *must* for a well-built Web site, especially if it's for business use. When the time comes to beta-test your site, bring in as rowdy and refractory a crowd as you can find. If you have picky customers (or colleagues who are pushy, opinionated, or argumentative), be comforted knowing that you have found a higher calling for them: Such people make ideal beta-testers — if you can get them to cooperate.

Don't wait till the very last minute to test your Web site. Sometimes the glitches found during the beta-test phase can take weeks to fix. Take heed: Test early and test often, and you'll thank us in the long run!

Beta-testers use your pages in ways you never imagined possible. They interpret your content to mean things you never intended in a million years. They drive you crazy and crawl all over your cherished beliefs and principles. And they do all this before your users do! Trust us, that's a blessing — even if it's in disguise.

These colleagues also find gotchas, big and small, that you never knew existed. They catch typos that word processors couldn't. They tell you things you left out and things that you should have omitted. They give you a fresh perspective on your Web pages, and they help you see them from extreme points of view.

The results of all this suffering, believe it or not, are positive. Your pages will be clearer, more direct, and more correct than they would have been had you tested them by yourself. (If you don't believe us, of course, you *could* try skipping this step. And when real users start banging on your site, forgive us if we don't watch.)

Cover all the bases with peer reviews

If you're a user with a simple home page or a collection of facts and figures about your private obsession, this tip may not apply to you. Feel free to read it anyway — it just might come in handy down the road.

If your pages express views and content that represent an organization, chances are, oh, *about 100 percent* that you should subject your pages to peer-and-management review before publishing them to the world. In fact, we recommend that you build reviews into each step along the way as you build your site — starting by getting knowledgeable feedback on such basic aspects as the overall design, writing copy for each page, and the final assembly of your pages into a functioning site. These reviews help you avoid potential stumbling blocks, such as unintentional off-color humor or unintended political statements. If you have any doubts about copyright matters, references, logo usage, or other important details, get the legal department involved. (If you don't have one, you may want to consider a little consulting help for this purpose.)

Building a sign-off process into reviews so you can prove that responsible parties reviewed and approved your materials is a good idea. We hope you don't have to be that formal about publishing your Web pages, but it's far, far better to be safe than sorry. (This process is best called *covering the bases*, or perhaps it's really covering something else? You decide.)

Use the best tools of the testing trade

When you grind through your completed Web pages, checking your links and your HTML, remember that automated help is available. If you visit the W3C HTML Validator at `http://validator.w3.org`, you'll be well on your way to finding computerized assistance to make your HTML pure as air, clean as the driven snow, and standards-compliant as, ah, *really well-written HTML.* (Do we know how to mix a metaphor, or what?)

Likewise, investigating link checkers covered earlier in the chapter is smart; use them regularly to check links on your pages. These faithful servants tell you if something isn't current, and tell you where to find links that need fixing.

Schedule site reviews

Every time you change or update your Web site, you should test its functionality, run a spell check, perform a beta test, and otherwise jump through important hoops to put your best foot forward online. But sometimes you'll

Text is easy to enhance and modify with features like these:

- Color-coded HTML
- Integrated spell checker
- Search-and-replace tools to update whole projects, folders, and files
- Internal HTML validation
- Extensive online help if you need to access documentation on HTML and other popular scripting languages

HomeSite helps you perform

- Project management
- Link verification
- File uploads to a remote Web server

HomeSite retails for $99, and works only on Windows, in case you think you might want to buy it. If you don't have HomeSite already, and don't want to fork out the cash, try one of the following challengers as your helper editor instead (note also that HomeSite comes bundled with Dreamweaver).

Contenders

There are many more good HTML helper editors than there are good WYSIWYG editors. Here's our slate of alternatives.

BBEdit/TextWrangler

BBEdit has ruled the Macintosh world for years. It comes in two versions:

- A free product formerly known as BBEdit Lite has been superseded by a newer, free text editor called TextWrangler.
- BBEdit ($200 retail)

   If you don't need the powerful and specialized set of HTML editing, preview, and cleanup tools that come with BBEdit, use TextWrangler and save! (A detailed features comparison is available online at www.barebones.com/ products/bbedit/threeway.shtml.)

If you use a Macintosh, check BBEdit out at www.barebones.com.

HTML-Kit

HTML-Kit is a compact Windows tool with

- Menu-driven support for both HTML and Cascading Style Sheets (CSS) markup
- A nice preview window for a browser's-eye view of your markup

If you want to download HTML-Kit, go to `www.chami.com/html-kit`. You can download a free version, or register your copy for $65 and obtain a bunch of extra tools — including a spiffy table designer, a log analyzer, and a nifty graphical HTML/XHTML/XML editor that lets you view and navigate all those documents through their syntactical structure.

WYSIWYG editors

A WYSIWYG editor creates markup for you as you create and lay out Web page content on your monitor (often by dragging and dropping visual elements, or working through GUI menus and options), shielding your delicate eyes from bare markup along the way. These tools are like word processors or page-layout programs; they do lots of work for you.

WYSIWYG editors make your work easier and save hours of endless coding — you have a life, right? — but you should only use WYSIWYG editors during the initial design stage. For example, you can use a WYSIWYG editor to create a complex table in under a minute during initial design work. Later, when the site is live, you would then use a helper to refine and tweak your HTML markup directly.

Dreamweaver: still the champ

Dreamweaver is the best WYSIWYG Web development tool for Macintosh and PC systems. Many (if not most) Web developers use Dreamweaver. Dreamweaver is an all-in-one product that supports

- Web-site creation
- Maintenance
- Content management

The current version is Adobe Dreamweaver cs3. It also belongs to a suite of products — Adobe Creative Suite 3, usually abbreviated cs3 — that work together to provide a full spectrum of Internet solutions. Adobe cs3 comes in many flavors — which include components such as InDesign, PhotoShop, Illustrator, Acrobat Professional, Dreamweaver, Fireworks, Contribute, After Effects Professional, Premiere Pro, Soundbooth, Encore, and even OnLocation. In fact, for a mere $2,500 or so, you can buy the Adobe Create Suite 3 Master Collection and get all of these things in a single (very expensive) box!

Dreamweaver features an easy-to-follow-and-learn GUI so you can style Web pages with CSS without even knowing what a style rule is! Many of the benefits of Dreamweaver stem from its sleek user interface and its respect for clean HTML. You can learn more about Dreamweaver by visiting the Adobe Web site at `www.adobe.com/products/dreamweaver`.

If you're too low on funds for a top-of-the-line WYSIWYG HTML editor like Dreamweaver cs3 (suggested retail price is about $400, but discounts of up to $200 are available), there are other possibilities. You can ponder the suggestions in the next section or go a-searching on the Web (the search string "WYSIWYG HTML editor" should do nicely) to find lots more still!

Contenders

WYSIWYG editors generate allegiances that can seem as pointless as the enmity between owners of Ford and Chevy trucks. All three of the following editors have fans, and all can both produce great Web pages.

- **Adobe GoLive** is a Web page editor that offers text and WYSIWYG editors, along with color coding, automatic code completion, HTML validation, nice site management chops, and bunches more. It lists for $400. Check it out at .

    www.adobe.com/products/golive

- **CoffeeCup HTML Editor 2007** is a Windows-based Web package that offers a code editor (text) and a visual editor (WYSIWYG), along with drag'n'drop scripting, support for pre-fab code elements called *snippets*, and a nifty image editor/mapper. It costs only $49. Check it out at

    www.coffeecup.com/html-editor/

- **HotDog Pro** is a compact, likeable HTML editor that operates in text and WYSIWYG modes. It, too, supports color coding, an HTML validator, offers lots of interesting image handling features, and even a slick multi-file find and replace/edit toolset. Take a bite at:

    www.sausage.com/hotdog-professional.html

Graphics Tools

Graphics applications are beasts. They can do marvelous things, but learning how to use them can be overwhelming at first.

If you aren't artistically inclined, consider paying someone else to do your graphics work. Graphics applications can be pricey and complicated. But you should have some kind of high-function (if not high-end) graphics program to tweak images should you need to. Our highest rating goes to Adobe Photoshop, but considering its cost and the average newbie HTML hacker's budget, we discuss a lower-cost alternative first in the following section.

Photoshop Elements: The amateur champ

At around $100 (with discounts as low as $80), Adobe Photoshop Elements 6.0 is an affordable PC- and Mac-based starter version of the full-blown Photoshop (the gold standard for graphics). You can do almost anything with Photoshop Elements that you might need for beginning and intermediate-level graphics editing.

This product is for you if you want to add images to your site but you don't want to work with graphics all the time, or use fancy special effects . To learn more about Photoshop Elements, visit www.adobe.com, select Products⇨ All Products, and then select whichever version of Photoshop Elements (PC or Mac) you want to read more about from the drop-down menu.

If you're really on a tight budget, check out the $90, PC-only Paint Shop Pro Photo X2 at www.corel.com instead. It does nearly everything that Photoshop does and costs less than Photoshop Elements.

Professional contenders

If you work with photographs or other high-resolution, high-quality images or artwork, you may need one of these Web graphics tools.

Adobe Photoshop

If it weren't so darned expensive, we'd grant top honors to Photoshop. Alas, $650 is too high for many novices' budgets. Wondering whether to upgrade from Photoshop Elements? Adobe mentions these capabilities among its "Top reasons to upgrade":

- **Improved file browser:** Shows and tells you more about more kinds of graphics files and gives you more-powerful search tools.

- **Shadow/Highlight correction:** Powerful built-in tools add or manipulate shadows and highlights in images.

- **More-powerful color controls:** Color palettes and color-matching tools with detailed controls that Elements lacks.

- **Text on a path:** Full-blown Photoshop lets you define any kind of path graphically and then instructs your text to follow that path. This capability supports fancy layouts that Elements can't match.